The Vietnam War
How the United States Became Involved

Edited and Introduced by
Mitch Yamasaki, Ph.D.

 Perspectives on History

HistoryCompass

Boston, Massachusetts

HistoryCompass
www.historycompass.com

© 2006 History Compass, LLC
  2nd edition

ISBN 1-932663-14-2 paperback edition
Library of Congress Catalog Card Number 96-86744

10   9   8   7   6   5   4   3   2   1

Printed in Canada

Subject Reference Guide:

THE VIETNAM WAR: How the United States Became Involved
edited by Mitch Yamasaki, Ph.D.

⇥Table of Contents⇤

Chronology

Trieu Au fought for Vietnam's independence against China in the 3rd century A.D. She was Vietnam's Joan of Arc.

(From: Center for Social Studies Education, *The Lessons of the Vietnam War*)

Introduction

by Mitch Yamasaki

Although the Vietnam War ended many years ago, questions about it continue to haunt the American people. What, for example, did the United States hope to accomplish in Vietnam? Why did America commit so many of its resources to a region of the world where it seemingly had so little interest? How did a poorly armed guerrilla army thwart the efforts of the most powerful country in the world? This text addresses these questions by (1) providing historical background, (2) analyzing a number of pertinent sources, and (3) examining the major interpretations of how and why the United States became involved in the Vietnam War.

❖❖❖

The Vietnamese People

In order to comprehend America's involvement in Vietnam, one must first understand the people of that country. The Vietnamese people originated from the Red River Valley near the Chinese border. They were conquered by the Chinese in 111 B.C.E. (B.C.) and ruled by them for over one thousand years. During that period, the Vietnamese adopted China's agricultural practices, writing system, clothing, hair styles and religious/philosophical system (consisting of Confucianism, Taoism, and Buddhism). They also adopted China's government institutions, including the emperor and his mandarin bureaucracy. In Vietnam, however, it was said that "the law of the emperor ends at the village gate." Autonomous and self-sufficient, the village was central to the lives of the Vietnamese people. Loyalty to one's family and village was far more important to a Vietnamese than his or her individuality. For a Vietnamese to lose his or her place in the village was equivalent to being without an identity. There is, as historian Frances Fitzgerald observed, no Vietnamese word that corresponds to the English word "I." Instead, "when a man speaks of himself, he calls himself 'your brother,' 'your nephew,' 'your teacher,' depending upon his relationship to the person he addresses." (Fitzgerald 28) (Full references for all citations found at page 78.) Wealth was not a sign of success in the traditional Vietnamese village, especially if it was acquired at the

VIETNAM AND MAINLAND SOUTHEAST ASIA
1954 – 1975

CHINA

Mandalay

NORTH VIETNAM

RED R.
MEKONG R.
RED R.

Dien Bien Phu

Hanoi

BURMA

Luang Prabang

Thanh Hoa

Haiphong

GULF OF TONKIN

HAINAN (CHINA)

Chiang Mai

Vientiane

L A O S

17º (PARTITION LINE) 1954-1975

Hue

Da Nang

Rangoon

THAILAND

Bangkok

Pleiku

CAMBODIA (KAMPUCHEA)

Phnom Penh

MEKONG R.

SOUTH VIETNAM

Cam Ranh

Saigon

(after 1975: Ho Chi Minh City)

Kompong Som

MEKONG DELTA

GULF OF THAILAND

ANDAMAN SEA

SOUTH CHINA SEA

N
W E
S

MALAYSIA

SUMATRA (INDONESIA)

MILES 300
0
KM 300
0

(From *America in Vietnam,* W. A. Williams et al., eds., Norton, 1989) expense of fellow villagers. Wealthy villagers were, in fact, expected to pay a higher share of the village's taxes and to financially support its banquets and festivals. Such practices had a leveling effect, so that as a proverb noted, "No family stays rich for three generations, and no family stays poor for three generations." The villager saw himself as a trustee or caretaker of his land rather than its "private property" owner. This belief persisted into the twentieth century. In 1968, at the height of the Vietnam War, American and South Vietnamese forces declared a small village in Quang Nam province a "free fire zone" and proceeded to evacuate its inhabitants. One old man refused to leave, saying "I have to guard [this land] for my grandson." "If I leave," he continued, "the graves of my ancestors... will become forest." (Fitzgerald 11) When the soldiers returned fourteen months later, they found the old man's body, buried in his land by artillery fire.

Although the Vietnamese people were deeply influenced by China's civilization, they fiercely retained their national identity. It is therefore not surprising that their most beloved heroes and heroines have been individuals who fought for Vietnam's independence. These include the Trung sisters, who led a revolt against the Chinese in the first century C.E. (A.D.); Tran Hung Dao, who drove the Mongols out of Vietnam in the thirteenth century; and Ho Chi Minh, who struggled against the French and the Americans in the twentieth century. When the powerful T'ang Dynasty in China collapsed (907 C.E.), the Vietnamese revolted and eventually drove out the Chinese in 939. Except for brief interludes, Vietnam maintained its independence for the next nine hundred years, despite threats from the Champa Kingdom to the south, the Khmer (Cambodian) Empire to the west, and China to the north. It was this prolonged struggle for a national identity, according to historian William Duiker, that "created in Vietnam a distinctly 'national' ethnic spirit, more self-conscious, and more passionate than that found virtually anywhere in Southeast Asia." (Duiker 16)

The Vietnamese began to migrate southward in the fifteenth century. They advanced slowly, reaching the Mekong River delta in the middle of the eighteenth century. Their migration was not peaceful. The Vietnamese destroyed the Champa Kingdom and took the best agricultural lands from the Chams and other ethnic groups, forcing many of them to live in isolated mountainous regions. In the twentieth century, the French and later the Americans would enlist these "montagnard" peoples to fight against their Vietnamese enemies.

The expansion strained the Vietnamese government and ultimately led to a breakup of the country. After a period of intrigues, rebellions, and civil wars, the Nguyen family reunited Vietnam in 1802.

French Rule

The first Europeans to arrive in Vietnam were Catholic missionaries in the late sixteenth century. Missionaries were fairly successful at attaining conversions but faced constant government persecution.

Nguyens enlisted the aid of Westerners in their struggle to reunify Vietnam. French missionaries provided supplies and recruited mercenaries for the Nguyens in hopes of gaining their support if they succeeded in reunifying the country. Unfortunately for the missionaries, the Nguyen emperors were deeply influenced by mandarins who saw the missionaries as threats to their authority. The mandarins persuaded the emperors to intensify their persecution of Christian missionaries and their converts. French missionaries urged their government to launch a military campaign to end the persecutions. French businessmen who saw economic opportunities in the region supported the call for military action. French forces attacked the Vietnamese port city of Danang in 1858. They managed to conquer all of Vietnam by 1883. The French also incorporated Cambodia (annexed in 1863) and Laos (annexed in 1893) into their new Indochina empire.

France divided Vietnam into three states: Tonkin in the north, Cochin China in the south, and Annam in the middle. The French governed Cochin China as a colony but maintained a facade of Vietnamese rule in Tonkin and Annam. They permitted the Nguyen dynasty to continue governing those states under French supervision.

French rule in Vietnam (1883-1954) was characterized by economic exploitation, cultural chauvinism, and political repression. The colonial government undertook massive building projects, including railroads, harbors, and canals. These public works, however, did not benefit most of the French and Vietnamese taxpayers who paid for them. Instead, they enabled a small group of French businessmen and plantation owners to make enormous profits exporting rice and rubber. These profits were rarely reinvested in Vietnam. A head tax on all Vietnamese men reduced their disposable income, while a government monopoly on salt, alcohol, and opium raised prices on those and related items. These policies hurt the poorest elements of Vietnamese society. Indebtedness and farm foreclosures soared. Many were forced to seek employment in French-owned plantations and mines under conditions resembling slavery. The extent of French economic exploitation can be gauged by the fact that while Vietnam's rice production quadrupled between 1880 and 1930, the individual peasant's rice consumption decreased during the same period.

Europeans justified their imperialism in the nineteenth century as a "white man's burden" to civilize backward peoples. The French assumed that every aspect of their culture was superior to Vietnamese culture. This was clearly illustrated in their educational policy. The Vietnamese people had achieved a high level of literacy, prior to colonization, through one-teacher village schools that numbered over 20,000 across the country. French officials abruptly changed written Vietnamese from Chinese characters to a romanized script *(quoc ngu)* without providing adequate schools to train the people in the new writing system. In 1930, for example, there were only fourteen government-certified secondary schools and one university in Vietnam. The result was mass illiteracy, which the French attributed to the backwardness of the Vietnamese people. The system did produce a small group of highly educated Vietnamese elites. They were children of prominent families schooled in the *lycées*, which were intended primarily for French children. Many of these elites, however, became disillusioned because they were excluded from higher positions in the colonial administration reserved for Frenchmen.

Politically, French colonial rule was far more repressive than that of its English and American counterparts. Unlike the English, who created seats in Parliament for their Indian subjects, or the Americans, who trained their Filipino subjects for eventual self-rule, the French excluded most of their Indochinese subjects from participating in their colonial governments. It is not surprising, therefore, that resistance to French rule began soon after their colonization of Indochina. The first revolts were led by mandarins attempting to restore the traditional imperial system. The backward-looking mandarins, however, had little to offer a people undergoing fundamental changes in a rapidly "modernizing" world. Phan Boi Chau was the first Vietnamese nationalist to relate the plight of his people to modernization. Using Japan as his model, Chau formed the Modernization Society, which sought to create a modern Vietnamese nation based on Western science, technology, and political theory. In 1908, the society organized mass demonstrations to protest high taxes. The French reacted swiftly with mass arrests. Chau was forced to flee to China. In 1927, urban intellectuals formed the Vietnam Nationalist Party — Viet Nam Quoc Dan Dang (VNQDD) — to promote Vietnamese independence. The VNQDD quickly concluded that only an armed uprising could free Vietnam from French rule. In 1930, the VNQDD called for a mass uprising of Vietnamese troops in the French colonial army. Only one garrison in northern Vietnam responded. The French quickly put down the uprising and executed the mutineers. They then imprisoned and executed hundreds of VNQDD members, effectively crushing the organization. There were numerous reasons for the failure of these early nationalist movements, the foremost being their inability or unwillingness to create a mass movement that included peasants and workers.

An organization that actively sought the support of peasants and workers was the Indochinese Communist Party. One of its early leaders was the enigmatic Ho Chi Minh. Son of a disgruntled government official, Ho came to believe that the key to Vietnam's independence lay in the West. Ho dropped out of his *lycée* in 1911 and sailed to the West. Working menial jobs to pay his way, Ho traveled to the United States, England, and France. Ho was in Paris at the end of World War I. There, he was deeply inspired by President Woodrow Wilson's call for respecting the self-determination of all peoples and nations — weak or powerful. Ho presented a petition at the Versailles Conference in 1919 to grant the people of Indochina self-rule. The petition was ignored by the victorious Allies (France, Great Britain, Italy, and the United States), but Ho's bold act made him a hero among the intelligentsia in Vietnam. Disillusioned by the Allies' cavalier attitude towards peoples living under colonial rule, Ho turned to communism. He became a founding member of the French Communist Party in 1920. In 1923, Ho traveled to the Soviet Union to receive training from the Comintern, an organization that promoted communist revolutions throughout the world. The Comintern sent Ho to China to work with the Chinese Nationalist Party (the Kuomintang). In China, Ho organized Vietnamese political exiles into the Vietnamese Revolutionary Youth Movement and helped found the Indochinese Communist Party in 1930. In Vietnam, Communist leaders such as Pham Van Dong (future prime minister of

North Vietnam) and Vo Nguyen Giap (future commander of the North Vietnamese army) engineered peasant uprisings and set up several people's "soviets" (village councils) in the early 1930s. These were quickly crushed by the French, who imprisoned, tortured, and executed thousands of peasants and revolutionaries. Giap's wife and sister-in-law were among those who were tortured and executed.

◆◆◆

World War II and Its Ramifications

French colonial rule in Indochina was dealt a major blow in 1940, when Japanese troops marched into Vietnam shortly after France's surrender to Nazi Germany. Left to fend for itself, the French colonial government capitulated to Japanese demands. The Japanese allowed the French to continue governing Indochina. In return, the French placed Indochinese military facilities and economic resources at Japan's disposal. This tenuous partnership lasted until 1945. By this time, Japan's war against the United States was going very badly. This made them wary of French treachery, especially after the liberation of France in 1944. In 1945, the Japanese arrested French officials and took direct control of Indochina. They had France's puppet emperor Bao Dai declare Vietnam "independent," which in effect made him their puppet.

Many Southeast Asian nationalists, such as Akmed Sukharno of Indonesia, had welcomed the Japanese as liberators. Ho Chi Minh, however, saw the Japanese as merely one colonial ruler replacing another. Ho's Indochina Communist Party inaugurated the Vietnam Independence League in 1941. Better known as the Vietminh, this organization had the goal of liberating Vietnam from both the French and the Japanese. Noncommunists joined the Vietminh. But from its inception, communists dominated its programs and operations. In 1945, with the French removed from power and the Japanese busy fighting a losing war, the Vietminh began to expand their operations. Starting at the village level, they came to control Vietnam's six northern provinces by the end of World War II.

During the war, the Vietminh saw themselves as part of a global struggle against fascism. They worked closely with the United States to defeat Japan, rescuing downed American pilots and providing valuable information to military intelligence officers of the Office of Strategic

Services (OSS). They hoped that collaboration with the United States during World War II would lead to its support of Vietminh objectives afterwards. The Vietminh had reason to be hopeful because President Franklin D. Roosevelt stated publicly in 1944 that he did not wish to see Indochina returned to France (Document 1). Instead, he suggested that Indochina be governed by an international trusteeship. However, pressures from France and England, America's strongest allies, forced Roosevelt to abandon his Indochina trusteeship plan (Document 2). Any chance of the United States supporting an independent Vietnam faded with Roosevelt's death on April 12, 1945. The United States, in fact, had no clear goals for Indochina at the time of Roosevelt's death, as evidenced by the mixed messages that Harry S. Truman received from his state department when he assumed the presidency (Document 3).

When Japan surrendered on August 15, 1945, Bao Dai tried to assert himself as the leader of a new Vietnamese nation. Bao Dai, however, had no popular support. The Vietminh, who had wide support among the people, called for a national insurrection. The "August Revolution" swept the Vietminh into power. Their supporters quickly took control of Vietnam's major cities — Hanoi on August 19, Hue on August 23, and Saigon on August 25. Bao Dai abdicated on August 30, and on September 2, Ho Chi Minh delivered Vietnam's Declaration of Independence in the name of the newly created nation — the Democratic Republic of Vietnam (Document 4).

The United States, aware of the impending conflict between the French and the Vietminh, tried to steer clear of it. America, for example, refused to take part in the surrender of Japanese troops in Indochina. The Allies therefore called on British troops from India to disarm and repatriate Japanese soldiers in southern Vietnam. Elements of the Chinese Nationalist army were dispatched to perform the same functions in northern Vietnam. The British, who were sensitive about their own colonial situation, did all they could to bring the French back into power in the South. They even rearmed Japanese prisoners of war and ordered them to hold key positions against Vietminh forces until French troops arrived. British troops withdrew from Vietnam when French soldiers took control of Saigon. Meanwhile, Chinese troops arriving in the North began to loot and pillage. With no one else to turn to, Ho negotiated with the French to remove the Chinese soldiers. By renouncing all their remaining concessions in China, the French were able to persuade the Chinese to withdraw from northern Vietnam. They then reached an accord with the Vietminh on March 6, 1946. France recognized the Vietminh's Democratic Republic of Vietnam as a "Free State having its own Government... forming part of the Indochinese Federation [which would be a part of] the French Union." This was to be a political relationship that loosely resembled the British commonwealth system. In return, the Vietminh agreed to the temporary stationing of French troops in the North. Ho received harsh criticism from his colleagues for cooperating with the French. Ho answered his critics with a history lesson:

> Don't you remember your history? The last time the Chinese came, they stayed 1,000 years. The French are foreigners. They are weak. Colonialism is dying. The white man is finished in Asia. But if the Chinese stay now, they will never go. (Starr 2:5)

✦✦✦

French-Vietminh War (1946-54) and the Seeds of U.S. Involvement

Negotiations to create an Indochinese federation failed because the French were determined to regain control over their former colony and the Vietminh were just as determined to gain independence from France. In his last meeting with French Prime Minister Georges Bidault, on September 14, 1946, Ho Chi Minh warned, "If we must fight, we will fight. You will kill ten of our men, and we will kill one of yours. Yet, in the end, it is you who will tire." (Olson 26) As talks broke down, fighting broke out. The French, with their superior equipment and firepower, quickly took control of the major cities and highways. The countryside, however, belonged to the Vietminh, who also controlled the roads when the sun went down.

The Vietminh sought international support in their struggle against the French. The Soviet Union was recovering from the devastation of World War II and was concerned mainly with eastern Europe. It was not likely to come to the Vietminh's aid. As a result, the Vietminh tried to get the United States and the United Nations to intervene. Ho wrote several letters to American leaders asking for assistance (Document 5).

None was answered because the United States did not recognize the Democratic Republic of Vietnam, the government Ho represented. In desperation, Ho assured American officials that his motive was nationalistic — to create an independent Vietnamese state — and not to advance the cause of international communism. He even offered the use of Cam Ranh Bay as an American naval base. The United States declined. Ironically, Cam Ranh Bay became America's largest base complex in the 1960s, by which time Ho and the United States had become mortal enemies.

It was understandable for the Vietminh to seek support from the United States in 1946, not only because of their ties during World War II, but because America had become the world's preeminent economic and military power. The United States was the only industrial power to emerge from World War II relatively unscathed. Germany and Japan were defeated and in ruins. England, France, and the Soviet Union, while victorious, were devastated by the war. Until these nations recovered, America dominated the world's economy. With only six percent of the world's population, the United States controlled over fifty percent of its wealth. At the end of World War II, the United States also had a monopoly on atomic weapons. Its military-industrial output soared above that of all other nations. The Soviet Union, which had lost over twenty million people during World War II, could match America's military might only by keeping most of its troops in arms after the war.

Many Americans, after World War II, believed that their nation had been irresponsible in adopting a policy of isolationism during the 1920s and 1930s. Some believed that this policy contributed to the rise of fascism in Italy, Germany, and Japan, which ultimately led to World War II. They now called on America to assume its responsibilities as a super-power. After all, as historian Stephen E. Ambrose pointed out, the United States had achieved a global status that few states in history had enjoyed:

In...1945 America's prestige, like its relative power in the world, had never been higher. The United States had provided the tools and the men to save Europe and Russia from Hitler. The United States had driven the Italians out of their African colonies and thrown the Japanese out of [Asia and the Pacific].... After World War II, the U.S. followed a policy of magnanimity towards the losers. In occupied Germany and Japan, the U.S. taught the ways of democracy. Ho Chi Minh hailed the Americans as the true friends of the oppressed of the earth. So did such dissimilar men as de Gaulle, Churchill, and on one occasion even Stalin himself. In a world full of hatred, death, destruction, deception, and double-dealing, the United States at the end of World War II was almost universally regarded as the disinterested champion of justice, freedom, and democracy. (Ambrose 50-51)

America was, it seemed, the shining example for all others to follow. For this reason, there were no widespread international or domestic protests when General Douglas MacArthur, commander of the occupation forces in Japan after World War II, brought in bureaucrats and academics from the United States to rewrite Japan's constitution along American lines. Trying to remold the world in its own image, however, proved frustrating for the United States because, as Ambrose noted, "Six percent of the world's population could not run the lives of the remaining 94 percent." (Ambrose 61)

What frustrated and frightened Americans the most was the growth of communism after World War II. The expansion actually began during the war with the Soviet army's liberation of eastern Europe from Nazi Germany. The Soviet Union continued to exert its influence in the region after the war. It intervened in Polish, Czechoslovakian, and Hungarian politics to insure that pro-Soviet governments were maintained in those countries. The Soviets defended their aggressive policy by pointing out that European armies invading Russia historically marched through eastern Europe, including Napoleon's army in 1812 and the German army in 1914 and 1941. The United States opposed the Soviet policy in eastern Europe, seeing it as tyrannical and reminiscent of Nazi Germany's aggressive foreign policy in the 1930s. It also feared that

Soviet domination of eastern Europe was merely a first step in its goal of world domination. As a result, the United States adopted a policy to "contain" the spread of communism wherever it threatened to expand. Thus began the Cold War. The United States assembled the North Atlantic Treaty Organization (NATO) in 1949 to defend western Europe against Soviet aggression. The Soviet Union countered by forming the Warsaw Pact to defend eastern Europe against NATO aggression. The Cold War spread from Europe to Asia, Africa, and the Americas. Both sides hardened their views and began to speak of the conflict in terms of a holy struggle between the forces of good and evil (Document 6).

Fears and frustrations of the Cold War eventually affected the domestic policies of the antagonists. In the United States, President Truman established the Civil Service Commission Loyalty Review Board to flush out communist sympathizers within the federal government. The House Committee on Un-American Activities (HUAC) coerced Hollywood studios to blacklist actors, screen writers, and directors suspected of communist activities. In this atmosphere of fear and suspicion, Senator Joseph R. McCarthy found a platform that would insure his reelection. McCarthy claimed that he had a list of 205 known communists employed by the state department. He had no such list. But that did not matter. The American people believed that their country had been infiltrated by communist agents. McCarthy launched a campaign to expose communists employed by the state department and the army. McCarthy accused Secretary of State Dean Acheson, a devout anticommunist, of hiring and protecting communists. He also implied that former Secretary of State General George C. Marshall was part of a world-wide communist conspiracy. Hundreds of people in the private and public sectors were accused of communist affiliations during the "McCarthy era." Many lost their jobs and their standing in the community. Almost all of the competent Asia experts in the state department lost their posts. This would come back to haunt the United States. In his memoir, former Secretary of Defense Robert S. McNamara noted that because of those purges, the Kennedy and Johnson administrations were forced to make key decisions regarding Vietnam in the 1960s without accurate and thoughtful assessments of the country and its neighbors. (McNamara 32-33) Despite the harm that it caused, few people spoke up against the government's anti-Communist campaigns, fearing that they would also be accused of being communists.

American officials were concerned about Ho Chi Minh's communist affiliations from the time that he began working with OSS officers in World War II. During the war, most officials minimized Ho's communist connections in light of his importance to the war effort. As animosities between the United States and the Soviet Union heightened after the war, attitudes toward Ho changed dramatically. The "loss" of China to the communists in 1949 and communist North Korea's invasion of noncommunist South Korea in 1950 led most American policymakers to believe that Ho and the Vietminh were part of a communist strategy to dominate Asia (Document 7). For Secretary of State Acheson, his suspicions about Ho were confirmed when China and the Soviet Union recognized the Democratic Republic of Vietnam in 1950. Consequently, he advised President Truman to request financial assistance for France's war efforts against the Vietminh. Congress appropriated $2.6 billion for military and economic aid to France in 1950.

Dwight D. Eisenhower, who succeeded Truman as president in 1953, promptly accepted the policy of aiding the French in Indochina. Eisenhower advanced the "domino theory," where the fall of Indochina would result in the communist takeover of Southeast Asia and ultimately threaten the entire Pacific basin (Document 8). As a result, the Eisenhower administration continued to increase its aid to France until the end of the war in 1954. By that time, the United States was funding 80 percent of France's military expenses.

◆◆◆

Dienbienphu

By 1953, the French people had lost their enthusiasm for "the dirty little war" in Indochina. The French therefore agreed to discuss a cease-fire with the Vietminh. As plans for peace talks got under way, both sides tried to strengthen their military positions. General Henri Navarre, commander of the French forces in Indochina, ordered 12,000 of his elite troops to take and hold Dienbienphu, a remote village on the Vietnam-Laos border. Navarre wanted to use Dienbienphu as an outpost to prevent Vietminh incursions into Laos and as a "mooring point" from which to launch attacks against them. He also hoped to lure the Vietminh into an open battle for the village. French leaders were confident that the Vietminh could not defeat a modern European force in a "conventional" battle. General Vo Nguyen Giap, the Vietminh commander, surrounded Dienbienphu with 35,000 troops, effectively cutting off the French garrison from outside help. Advisers from the People's Republic of China, which supplied the Vietminh with arms and equipment, suggested "human wave" attacks. These resulted in heavy loses. Giap therefore ordered his soldiers to dig tunnels towards the French bases in the village. By April 1954 these tunnels came within a few yards of the bases. In fierce hand-to-hand fighting that followed, one French base after another fell to the Vietminh.

As the French situation at Dienbienphu deteriorated, they sent a delegation to Washington, D.C. to request massive American air strikes against Vietminh positions around the village. They warned that if the United States did not intervene immediately, the French would be driven out of Indochina, exposing the region to a communist takeover. This placed the Eisenhower administration in a quandary. It was determined to keep Indochina out of communist hands. However, after the Korean War experience, it did not wish to get involved in another land war in Asia. In the end, Eisenhower decided not to intervene for several key reasons. First, there was little prospect that air strikes alone could save Dienbienphu. Use of tactical nuclear weapons was discussed but quickly dismissed. This meant that American ground troops would also have to be sent in. The army estimate of how many soldiers would be needed to defeat the Vietminh was staggering. Army Chief of Staff General Matthew Ridgway predicted that over 500,000 would be required. Second, Eisenhower was not willing to commit American forces without Congressional support. Many influential Congressmen, including Senate Majority Leader Lyndon B. Johnson, opposed military intervention. Johnson stated that he could not support sending American soldiers "into the mud and muck of Indochina on a blood-letting spree to perpetuate colonialism and the white man's exploitation of Asia." (Starr 2:10) Third, both Eisenhower and Congress were reluctant to commit American forces without international support. Great Britain, America's longtime ally, was crucial to any "united action." The British, however, flatly refused to participate in any military operations. Fourth, the Eisenhower administration was committed to a foreign policy that emphasized nuclear deterrence while reducing conventional forces. A diversion of military resources to Indochina could undermine that global strategy by taking resources away from Europe and other regions that the United States saw as more vital in 1954. Finally, if the United States were to intervene, the Eisenhower administration demanded that France establish a definite timetable for granting Vietnam its independence. It also insisted that Americans be directly involved in the training and deployment of Vietnamese forces. The French refused because that would mean giving up what they were fighting to preserve — sovereignty over France's colonial empire.

‾‾‾‾‾‾‾‾‾‾‾‾‾‾‾‾‾‾‾‾‾‾ ◆◆◆ ‾‾‾‾‾‾‾‾‾‾‾‾‾‾‾‾‾‾‾‾‾‾

The Geneva Conference

America's decision not to intervene doomed the French garrison at Dienbienphu. It surrendered on May 7, 1954, after 55 days of courageous but hopeless combat. On the following day, delegates from the Soviet Union, Great Britain, the People's Republic of China, France, the United States, and the Democratic Republic of Vietnam met in Geneva to begin discussions on the future of Indochina. Delegates from the French-supported Royal Government of Laos, Royal Government of Cambodia, and the State of Vietnam also attended but did not play significant roles at the conference. The goal of the Geneva conference was to establish "a lasting peace" in the region. Various delegations, however, disagreed on how this was to be achieved (Document 9). After much discussion, a settlement was reached in July 1954. The French and the Vietminh agreed to a cease-fire, and the country was temporarily divided at the 17th parallel. The Vietminh would regroup to the north of that line, while forces loyal to the French would regroup south of it. The agreement also called for elections to be held within two years to reunite the country.

The United States saw the creation of a communist North Vietnam as a threat to the region and refused to sign the Geneva accords. American delegate Walter B. Smith pledged to abide by their terms, but President Eisenhower later announced that the United States was not bound to honor the accords. In September 1954, the United States formed the Southeast Asian Treaty Organization (SEATO) along with France, Great Britain, Australia, New Zealand, Pakistan, Thailand, and the Philippines. Members agreed to "maintain and develop their individual and collective capacity to resist armed attack and to prevent...subversive activities directed against their territorial integrity and political stability." (Williams 175) A protocol extended SEATO's protection to Laos, Cambodia and Vietnam south of the 17th parallel. SEATO therefore provided the "legal" basis for America's involvement in Vietnam after the Geneva conference.

(By Edmund Valtmna, appeared in the *Hartford Times,* October 2, 1965, Lyndon Baines Johnson Library, National Archives)

Ngo Dinh Diem

In 1954, Ngo Dinh Diem became premier of South Vietnam (called the State of Vietnam until 1955, when it was renamed the Republic of Vietnam). Diem came from a prominent Catholic family in Hue. He had considered the priesthood before turning to politics. Diem's strengths were his honesty and fairness. His weaknesses were his stubbornness and self-righteousness. Diem also lacked strong bonds of loyalty and respect as a patriotic leader from the people of South Vietnam — which his Vietminh counterparts in the North enjoyed — because he did not take part in the struggle against the French. American officials were initially skeptical about Diem. They were, however, impressed with Diem's determination to prevent a communist takeover of Vietnam. American officials also did not find any other South Vietnamese leader they could support.

Diem faced monumental problems when he became premier. Aside from the Vietminh that did not migrate to the North, Diem had to deal with militant religious sects, rebellious generals, and a river pirate who controlled Saigon's police force. Diem alienated many people when he settled Catholic immigrants from the North in prime agricultural lands after displacing Buddhist farmers who had lived in those regions for generations. In 1956, he outraged large segments of the population by refusing to hold elections to reunite Vietnam, as mandated by the Geneva accords. The United States supported Diem's decision because it feared that Ho Chi Minh would emerge victorious if elections were held at that time. With American support, Diem was able to overcome his major rivals in South Vietnam. In the process, however, his regime became increasingly repressive. Diem called all of his opponents "Vietcong," regardless of their ideological orientation, and attempted to eliminate all of them. He arrested tens of thousands of political activists and held them in concentration camps. Farmers were forced to attend mass meetings where they were ordered to expose the Vietcong and their sympathizers. Diem's opponents retaliated by assassinating his officials, especially those at the village level. Many joined the National Liberation Front (NLF). Founded in 1960, the NLF was made up of a wide range of anti-Diem groups but was led and controlled by southern communists with ties to North Vietnam. Its chief (and unifying) goal was to overthrow Diem. As opposition to his regime grew, Diem trusted fewer and fewer people. Towards the end of his rule, Diem trusted only his relatives, in particular his ambitious brother and sister-in-law — Ngo Dinh Nhu and Madame Nhu. Among other posts, Diem appointed Nhu head of his security forces.

North Vietnamese leaders were initially hesitant about supporting southern insurgents, concerned that it would disrupt their badly needed economic development programs. They also feared that it would trigger an escalation in the American involvement in Vietnam. This changed when Le Duan, a communist leader from the South, became a leading official in the North Vietnamese government. He convinced northern leaders that aiding southern insurgents was vital to their own interests. In 1960, the Vietnam Communist Party Congress declared that its "two priorities" were "to carry out the socialist revolution in the North [and] to liberate the South from the rule of the American imperialists and their henchmen [enabling the Vietnamese people to] achieve national reunification." (Kahin 114-15) This paved the way for northern communists, especially former Vietminh who had migrated from the South after the Geneva Conference, to infiltrate into South Vietnam to help overthrow Diem's regime. The numbers infiltrating were small in the early 1960s but increased as American support of the South Vietnamese government escalated.

◆◆◆

The Kennedy Administration and the Vietnam War

When John F. Kennedy was elected president in 1960, he assembled a remarkable team of advisers — the nation's "best and brightest." (Document 10) Coming from the nation's elite universities and major corporations, they were, according to journalist David Halberstam, "men of force, not cruel, not harsh, but men who acted rather than waited." (Halberstam 50) These men would shape the Kennedy and Johnson administrations' policies towards Vietnam. Initially impressed by them, Halberstam eventually came to see their elitism — the belief that they always knew what was best for the country, more so than its people — as the roots of America's tragic involvement in Vietnam.

Emerging from the politics of the McCarthy era, President Kennedy felt he had to prove that he was not "soft on communism." "Let every nation know," Kennedy declared in his 1961 inaugural address, "that we shall pay any price, bear any burden, meet any hardship, support any friend, oppose any foe to assure the survival and the success of liberty." Kennedy, however, was embarrassed shortly after his inauguration by the ill-fated Bay of Pigs invasion designed to overthrow Fidel Castro's government in Cuba. Later that year, he was bullied by Soviet Premier Nikita Khrushchev in their meeting in Vienna. Kennedy also inherited "a mess" in Laos, where America's efforts to establish an anticommunist government resulted in numerous coups and factional conflicts. He opted for a political solution (rather than a military one) in Laos, allowing the major factions, including the communist Pathet Lao, to form a neutralist coalition government.

After the Bay of Pigs fiasco, the intimidation in Vienna, and the Laotian compromise, Kennedy had to take a stand somewhere if his Cold War rhetoric was to be taken seriously. Vietnam became that place. In order to stabilize Diem's deteriorating regime, Kennedy increased the number of American military personnel stationed in Vietnam from less than 700 to over 16,000 during his presidency. As a senator, Kennedy had criticized the Eisenhower administration for intervening in countries like Vietnam, because it failed to recognize the appeal of indigenous nationalist movements for peoples living under oppressive colonial governments. As president, Kennedy criticized Eisenhower's foreign policy on strategic rather than moral grounds. He believed that reliance on nuclear weapons was ineffective for fighting "wars of national liberation," which were usually guerrilla wars. Kennedy therefore adopted a "flexible response," which included (1) using special forces (Green Beret) troops; (2) providing the Army of the Republic of Vietnam (ARVN) increased training, fire-power and technological support; (3) conducting covert operations led by Central Intelligence Agency (CIA) officers; (4) encouraging humanitarian efforts to win over the "hearts and minds" of the Vietnamese people; and (5) initiating the "strategic hamlet" program. Modeled after the successful British counterinsurgency strategy in Malaya, the strategic hamlet program sought to isolate the Vietcong from their food supplies, hiding places, and sources of recruitment by moving peasants into villages secured by government troops.

Despite these efforts, the situation in South Vietnam continued to deteriorate. One reason was because enhanced training, mobility, and fire-power did not significantly improve the ARVN's fighting ability. American advisers generally trained government troops to fight conventional forces, which the Vietcong were not. Green Beret advisers taught some guerrilla tactics but tactics alone could not fix the ARVN's fundamental problems. ARVN officers were chosen for their loyalty to Diem rather than their military abilities. Many were northern Catholics who migrated to the South after the Geneva conference. Corruption was rampant among ARVN officers, who were enticed by the enormous aid that came in from the United States. As American aid to South Vietnam increased, power and prestige gravitated from civil officials to military officers, reflecting the imbalance of military versus "humanitarian" aid being sent there. ARVN's enlisted soldiers were nearly all draftees. Most were Buddhist peasants. They had nothing to fight for in the South Vietnamese army. Draft dodging and desertions were therefore chronically high. The ARVN's casualty rates were usually low in the early 1960s, not because of its military prowess, but because its units avoided combat whenever possible. Government troops also tended to alienate villagers rather than win over their hearts and minds. Well-equipped and well-supplied by the Americans, ARVN soldiers did not depend on the villagers. As a result, they treated peasants with disdain and disrespect. The Vietcong, on the other hand, depended on villagers to hide and feed them. There were abuses of peasants by both sides, but the Vietcong were likely to treat villagers more "politely and nicely" than ARVN soldiers. Peasants trusted and supported the Vietcong more than the ARVN, not only because they treated peasants better, but because people tend to trust those who depend on them more than those who do not. Second, air power was not effective against guerrilla forces that disappeared into the jungle. In addition, bombing often turned peasants against the Saigon government, especially when bombs fell on their villages. Third, villagers regarded Diem's officials as outsiders and treated them with suspicion. Most peasants saw Americans, not as saviors, but as new western imperialists replacing old ones (the French). Their joint efforts to capture the hearts and minds of the Vietnamese peasants therefore usually failed. Finally, the strategic hamlet program alienated Vietnamese peasants by removing them from their traditional lands, placing them in remote regions and restricting their travel into and out of their new hamlets.

By 1963, the NLF controlled most of the villages in South Vietnam. General Paul D. Harkins, the American commander in Vietnam, however, continued to send the Kennedy administration optimistic reports on the progress being made by Diem's government and ARVN forces. American field advisers, such as Lieutenant Colonel John Paul

Vann, who reported the failures of the South Vietnamese forces were silenced. A crisis erupted in 1963, however, which could not be kept quiet. It began when government security forces, under Ngo Dinh Nhu's orders, broke up peaceful gatherings to celebrate the Buddha's birthday. In protest marches that followed, government soldiers shot and killed several demonstrators. A Buddhist monk, Thich Quang Duc, expressed his outrage by setting himself on fire near a busy intersection in Saigon. His martyrdom crystallized the resentment of many South Vietnamese toward the Diem regime. Thousands took to the streets, calling for Diem's and Nhu's removal. Several protesters emulated Duc's martyrdom. Nhu responded with mass arrests and attacks on Buddhist pagodas. Madame Nhu aggravated the situation by publicly ridiculing the protesters and martyrs.

News of these events reached the United States and embarrassed the Kennedy administration, which had helped to build up Diem's repressive regime. At the height of this crisis, a group of South Vietnamese generals approached CIA officers to discuss their plans to oust Diem. The main concern of the generals was whether the United States would support their regime after a successful coup. The Kennedy administration was split on the coup (Document 11). Some of Kennedy's advisers believed that Diem would have to be replaced if South Vietnam was to survive. Other advisers felt that eliminating Diem would destabilize the South Vietnamese government and cause it to fall. The Kennedy administration initially tried to avert a coup by urging Diem to curb the violence against protesters and to enact reforms which would make his government more inclusive. It also recommended that Diem remove Nhu from his government. Diem made some gestures toward reform but refused to remove his brother. Meanwhile, Nhu hinted that he was negotiating with North Vietnam to form a neutralist government similar to Laos's. French President Charles de Gaulle, who offered to arrange the negotiations, stated that the creation of a neutralist government was the best way to end the conflict in Vietnam. Frustrated and unsettled by these developments, the Kennedy administration approved the coup and pledged support to the generals afterwards. In early November 1963, the generals carried out the long anticipated coup, killing Diem and Nhu in the process.

President Johnson and the Escalation of American Involvement

Kennedy himself was assassinated within weeks of Diem's death. Historians still debate over what Kennedy would have done about Vietnam if he had not been assassinated. Some feel he would have escalated America's involvement, while others believe he would have withdrawn from Vietnam. "Whatever his fears or his ultimate intentions," historian George C. Herring notes that Kennedy "bequeathed to his successor a problem eminently more dangerous than the one he had inherited from Eisenhower." (Herring 107) Lyndon B. Johnson was a man of enormous power, drive and political savvy. He also possessed deep insecurities, stemming from his poor, southern background. This combination produced a president whose accomplishments and failures will be debated by historians for many decades. As president, Johnson's main concerns were domestic (and primarily social) — anti-poverty and civil rights programs designed to create his "Great Society." He did not wish to get entangled in a war in Asia, especially if it would interfere with his domestic programs. However, like his predecessors, Johnson did not want to seem "soft on communism." Also, as vice president, Johnson visited South Vietnam in 1961 and gave his word that America would continue its commitment to the country. "I am not going to lose Vietnam," he told Henry Cabot Lodge, Jr., America's ambassador to South Vietnam, "I am not going to be the President who saw Southeast Asia go the way China went." (Halberstam 364) Johnson's determination to carry out his massive social programs *and* fight to preserve the South Vietnamese government in time clashed and ultimately destroyed his presidency.

During his first year as president, Johnson carried on Kennedy's policies toward South Vietnam — providing economic assistance, military supplies, army advisers, and CIA operatives. Johnson relied on Kennedy's advisers, most of whom he retained, to take care of Vietnam while he focused on his domestic agenda. One operation developed by the CIA at this time used American vessels to identify North Vietnamese coastal installations which would later be attacked by South Vietnamese commandos. An American destroyer, the *Maddox*, was part of such a mission when it was attacked by North Vietnamese PT boats in the Gulf of Tonkin on August 1, 1964. The United States immediately warned North Vietnam that it would retaliate if attacks on American vessels persisted. On August 4, two American destroyers patrolling the same area, the *Maddox* and the *C. Turner Joy*, reported being attacked by enemy vessels. After reviewing the ships' reports, some of Johnson's advisers doubted that the destroyers were actually attacked. Regardless of these doubts, Johnson ordered retaliatory air strikes against North Vietnamese naval bases. On August 5, Johnson had his longtime political ally Senator J. William Fulbright introduce what came to be called the Gulf of Tonkin Resolution (Document 12). It gave the president the power "to take all necessary measures to repel any armed attack against the forces of the United States and to prevent further aggression." The Johnson administration did not inform Congress that the *Maddox* was part of a covert operation against North Vietnam when it was attacked on August 1. Nor did it tell Congress that evidence on the alleged attacks on the *Maddox* and the *Turner Joy* on August 4 were inconclusive. Congress therefore saw the resolution as a reasonable response to "unprovoked" attacks on American vessels and passed it with almost no debate. Johnson was delighted. The resolution showed that both he and Congress were determined to "stand firm" against communist aggression. It also gave Johnson a free hand to conduct military operations in Vietnam (without further Congressional approval). "The resolution," Johnson later told an aid, "was like grandma's nightshirt — it covered everything."

Meanwhile in Vietnam, several coups rocked the Saigon government and further destabilized the country. Generals ousted their rivals from power, only to be driven out themselves by other generals. None of these regimes gained the support of the South Vietnamese people. Ironically, the NLF (Vietcong) encountered recruitment problems after Diem's and Nhu's deaths. With their deaths, the NLF lost the targets of the Vietnamese peoples' resentment. This slack was taken up by soldiers of the North Vietnam Army (NVA) infiltrating from the North. It did not matter whether ARVN forces were fighting the NLF or the NVA. They did badly against both. By the end of 1964, Johnson's advisers were telling him that unless the United States escalated its involvement in Vietnam the Saigon regime would fall. Johnson, however, was not sure that the United States should escalate. He met secretly with his advisers to discuss his options (Document 13). One option that emerged was to Americanize the war and begin an all-out effort to defeat the enemy.

LBJ showing his scar shaped like a map of Vietnam, by David Levine
(From the *New York Review of Books, 1966,* courtesy of the National Archives)

A second option was to escalate America's involvement incrementally, assessing each step before moving to the next. A third option was to stop the escalation, negotiate a settlement, and gradually withdraw. A fourth option was to pull out of Vietnam immediately.

Johnson rejected the first option because of the probable loss of American lives and the possibility of a Soviet/Chinese intervention. He rejected option four because that would mean going back on America's commitments to the South Vietnamese government. Johnson also did not want to be "the first American president to lose a war." He could not accept option three because negotiations would mean accepting a coalition government for South Vietnam which included the NLF. Johnson believed that such a government would be dominated by the NLF, which would try to unite the country with North Vietnam. This would mean a "defeat" for the United States. Johnson therefore saw option two as the only viable course of action (Document 14). Johnson believed that with this option he could control the pace and direction of the conflict. He was wrong.

Johnson's escalation of the war began with bombing. Earlier studies showed that bombing did not deter a determined enemy. They revealed, for example, that the massive bombing of German cities during World War II did not significantly slow down the country's war production. Instead, it rallied the angry German people behind their nation's war efforts. If bombing had little effect on an industrialized nation such as Nazi Germany, its effect on a predominantly agricultural country like Vietnam was sure to be minimal. Walt Rostow, assistant national security director, was nevertheless convinced that bombing would bring the United States victory. Few members of Johnson's administration agreed with Rostow's assessment, but they recommended bombing because it was the safest way to escalate the war. Bombing missions posed minimal risks to American lives. Johnson therefore authorized a gradually expanding bombing campaign against North Vietnam, while enlarging the air war in South Vietnam. Before the war was over, the United States would drop more bombs on that little country than on the Asian and European theatres of World War II.

A few weeks after the bombing campaign began, General William Westmoreland, who replaced General Harkins as commander of American forces in Vietnam, requested Marine combat units to defend the American air base in Danang. Westmoreland justified his request

"...Meanwhile Back On The Home Front,"
by Gene Basset, *Scripps-Howard News Service,* November 1, 1965,
National Archives

by indicating that he could not rely on ARVN forces to perform this duty. His request was approved, and two Marine battalions landed in Vietnam on March 8, 1965. This was a small but significant step. Once American combat troops landed in Vietnam, it became difficult for Johnson and his advisers to deny Westmoreland's requests for more troops, especially when the rationale for the increase involved saving the lives of American soldiers. The policy of using American troops to defend air bases led to "search and destroy" missions, with the idea that such operations expanded the defense perimeters of American outposts. American forces also took on the task of stopping the flow of NVA troops into South Vietnam. In July 1965, the Johnson administration approved sending an additional 50,000 combat troops to Vietnam. By the end of 1965, there were 190,000 American soldiers serving in Vietnam. The number rose to 400,000 in 1966 and to 500,000 in 1967. It topped off at 540,000 in 1968. From that year onward, the number of American troops in Vietnam steadily declined, although America's bombing campaign intensified and expanded to Laos and Cambodia. America's involvement in Vietnam dragged on even beyound 1973, when it signed a truce with the North Vietnamese government. The last American troops to leave Vietnam were Marines guarding the United States embassy in Saigon when the city fell to North Vietnamese troops in 1975. In some ways, America's withdrawal from Vietnam was as long and torturous as the process by which it became involved in the country.

Sources

DOCUMENT 1: Roosevelt's Trusteeship Plan for Indochina

Franklin D. Roosevelt championed anti-colonialism during his presidency. He therefore did not wish to see Indochina returned to France after World War II. Roosevelt made this clear in a memo to Secretary of State Cordell Hull, dated January 24, 1944:

> I saw Halifax [British Ambassador to the United States] last week and told him quite frankly that it was perfectly true that I had, for over a year, expressed the opinion that Indo-China should not go back to France but that it should be administered by an international trusteeship. France has had that country— thirty million inhabitants for nearly one hundred years, and the people are worse off than they were at the beginning.... France has milked it for one hundred years. The people of Indo-China are entitled to something better than that. (Williams 30)

◆◆◆

DOCUMENT 2: Allies' Responses to Roosevelt's Trusteeship Plan

At a February 23, 1945 press conference, a reporter asked Roosevelt who supported his trusteeship plan. His answer was that "Stalin liked the idea. China liked the idea. The British don't like it.... The French have talked about how they expect to recapture Indo-China, but they haven't got any shipping to do it with." Another reporter asked if British Prime Minister Winston Churchill "wants them [the Allies' colonies] all back just the way they were?" Roosevelt replied, "Yes, he is mid-Victorian on all things like that." (Williams 31)

Roosevelt's position on Indochina did not endear him to French leaders. In a March 13, 1945 memo to Secretary of State Hull, Jefferson Caffery, United States Ambassador to France, recounted his conversation with General Charles de Gaulle:

> General de Gaulle...said...that several expeditionary forces
> for Indochina had been prepared: Some troops were in North
> Africa, some in southern France and some in Madagascar,
> and the British had promised to transport them but at the last
> minute they were given to understand that owing to American
> insistence they could not transport them.... "This worries me
> a great deal...we do not understand your policy. What are you
> driving at?" (Williams 61)

De Gaulle warned Caffery that America's policy on Indochina could
drive France into the Soviet camp as the European theatre of the war
drew to a close:

> "Do you want us to become...one of the federated states
> under the Russian aegis? The Russians are advancing apace as
> you well know. When Germany falls they will be upon us. If
> the public here comes to realize that you are against us in
> Indochina there will be terrific disappointment and nobody
> knows to what that will lead. We do not want to become
> Communist; we do not want to fall into the Russian orbit, but
> I hope that you do not push us into it." (Williams 61-62)

✦✦✦

DOCUMENT 3: State Department Divided on Indochina Policy in 1945

When Harry S. Truman became president in April 1945, the U.S.
State Department was divided on what America's policy towards
Indochina should be. On April 20, 1945, the department's European
Affairs Division sent a memorandum to Truman with the following
recommendations:

> The Government of the United States should neither oppose the restoration of Indo-China to France, with or without a program of international accountability, nor take any action toward French overseas possessions which it is not prepared to take or suggest with regard to the colonial possessions of our other Allies....
>
> French offers of military and naval assistance in the Pacific should be considered on their merits as bearing upon the objective of defeating Japan, as in the case of British and Dutch proposals. The fact that acceptance of a specific proposal might serve to strengthen French claims for the restoration of Indo-China to France should not be regarded as grounds for rejection.... (Porter 40-41)

The Far East Division sent Truman a memo on the following day. While acknowledging French sovereignty in Indochina, the Far East Division warned Truman that if the United States did not insist on France extending some measure of self-government to the people of Indochina it might later be drawn into a conflict in the region:

> ...because without recognition of the dynamic trends towards self-government among the peoples of Asia there can be no peace and stability in the Far East and the peoples of Southeast Asia may embrace ideologies contrary to our own or develop a pan-Asiatic movement against all western powers, FE [Far Eastern Division] believes that it would not be unreasonable for the United States to insist that the French give adequate assurances as to the implementing of policies in Indochina which we consider essential to assure peace and stability in the Far East....
>
> If really liberal policies towards Indochina are not adopted by the French — policies which recognize the paramount interest of the native peoples and guarantee within the foreseeable future a genuine opportunity for true, autonomous self-government — there will be substantial bloodshed and unrest for many years, threatening the economic and social progress and the peace and stability of Southeast Asia. (Porter 43-45)

DOCUMENT 4: Vietnamese Declaration of Independence

Following Japan's surrender on August 15, 1945, the Vietminh and their supporters took control of Vietnam's major cities. On August 30, Emperor Bao Dai abdicated. Over 500,000 people gathered in Hanoi on September 2 to hear Ho Chi Minh's declaration of Vietnam's independence. As he spoke, American planes flew overhead in a display of friendship. At the end of Ho's speech, the Vietnamese band played the "Star-Spangled Banner":

All men are created equal. They are endowed by their Creator with certain inalienable rights; among these are Life, Liberty, and the pursuit of Happiness.

This immortal statement was made in the Declaration of Independence of the United States of America in 1776. In a broader sense, this means: All the peoples of the earth are equal from birth, all the peoples have a right to live, to be happy and free.

The Declaration of the French Revolution made in 1791 on the Rights of Man and the Citizen also states: "All men are born free and with equal rights, and must always remain free and have equal rights."

Those are undeniable rights.

Nevertheless, for more than eighty years, the French imperialists, abusing the standard of Liberty, Equality, and Fraternity, have violated our Fatherland and oppressed our fellow-citizens. They have acted contrary to the ideals of humanity and justice....

The French have fled, the Japanese have capitulated, Emperor Bao Dai has abdicated. Our people have broken the chains which for nearly a century have fettered them and have won independence for the Fatherland....

The whole Vietnamese people, animated by a common purpose, are determined to fight to the bitter end against any attempt by the French colonialists to reconquer their country.

continued

> We are convinced that the Allied nations, which at Tehran and San Francisco have acknowledged the principles of self-determination and equality of nations, will not refuse to acknowledge the independence of Vietnam.
>
> A people who have courageously opposed French domination for more than eighty years, a people who have fought side by side with Allies against the Fascists during these last years, such a people must be free and independent.... (Moss 32-33)

◆◆◆

DOCUMENT 5: Ho Chi Minh Asks for U.S. Support

When a showdown with the French became imminent in 1946, the Vietminh sought support from the world's major powers. Getting no response from the Soviet Union, Ho Chi Minh turned to the United States and the United Nations for help. Ho wrote seven letters to President Truman and Secretary of State James F. Byrnes, none of which was answered because the United States did not recognize Ho's government. Typical of these letters was one addressed to President Truman dated February 16, 1946:

> Our VIETNAM people, as early as 1941, stood by the Allies' side and fought against the Japanese and their associates, the French colonialists.
>
> From 1941 to 1945 we fought bitterly, sustained by the patriotism of our fellow-countrymen and by the promises made by the Allies at YALTA, SAN FRANCISCO AND POTSDAM.
>
> When the Japanese were defeated in August 1945, the whole Vietnam territory was united under a Provisional Republican Government which immediately set out to work. In five months, peace and order were restored, a democratic republic was established on legal bases, and adequate help was given to the Allies in the carrying out of their disarmament mission.
>
> But the French colonialists, who had betrayed in war-time both the Allies and the Vietnamese, have come back and are

continued

waging on us a murderous and pitiless war in order to reestablish their domination....

This aggression is contrary to all principles of international law and to pledges made by the Allies during the World War. It is a challenge to the noble attitude shown before, during and after the war by the United States Government and People....

The French aggression on a peace-loving people is a direct menace to world security. It implies complicity, or at least, the connivance of the Great Democracies. The United Nations ought to keep their words. They ought to interfere to stop this unjust war, and to show that they mean to carry out in peace-time the principles for which they fought in war-time.... It is with this firm conviction that we request of the Untied States as guardians and champions of World Justice to take a decisive step in support of our independence....We will do our best to make this independence and cooperation profitable to the whole world. (Porter 95)

◆◆◆

DOCUMENT 6: Truman Describes the Opposing Sides of the Cold War

As the Cold War began to heat up, American policymakers began to portray it in terms of a holy struggle between good and evil. This can be seen in President Truman's address to Congress on March 12, 1947:

At the present moment in world history nearly every nation must choose between alternative ways of life. One way of life is based upon the will of the majority, and is distinguished by free institutions, representative government, free elections, guarantees of individual liberty, freedom of speech and religion, and freedom from political oppression. The second way of life is based upon the will of a minority forcibly imposed on the majority. It relies upon terror and oppression, a controlled press and radio, fixed elections, and

continued

the suppression of personal freedoms. It must be the policy of the United States to support free peoples who are resisting attempted subjugation by armed minorities or by outside pressures.

American financier Bernard Baruch observed that Truman's address "was tantamount to a declaration of...an ideological or religious war." Journalist Walter Lippmann saw the policy that Truman outlined as a "strategic monstrosity," which could embroil the United States in disputes at the far corners of the world. As the Cold War intensified, however, few Americans would challenge Truman's view of the world. Truman's administration, in fact, would be accused of being "soft on communism."

◆◆◆

DOCUMENT 7: Changing Views of Ho Chi Minh by American Officials

Ho Chi Minh's communist affiliations were a concern to American officials from the outset. During World War II, however, most officials minimized Ho's communism in light of his importance to the Vietnamese people. "Whether we like the particular economic system or social system that he might develop or not," Assistant Secretary of State Thruston Morton noted, "we must remember that [Ho] is, indeed, considered by many peasants, the small people...as the George Washington of his country." (Starr 2:7) As the Cold War heated, however, American officials came to see Ho as a pawn in the Soviet-Chinese goal of dominating Asia. This was the conclusion reached by Secretary of State Dean Acheson, as indicated by a speech he gave in 1949:

[The] question [of] whether Ho [is] as much nationalist as commie is irrelevant. All Stalinists in colonial areas are nationalists. With the achievement [of] national aims (i.e. independence), their objectives necessarily become subordination [of the] state to commie purposes and [the] ruthless extermination not only [of] opposition groups but [of] all elements suspected [of] even [the] slightest deviation. (Starr 2:8)

✦✦✦

DOCUMENT 8: Eisenhower Advances the Domino Theory

Dwight D. Eisenhower, who succeeded Truman as president in 1953, promptly accepted the policy of aiding France in Indochina. In an April 7, 1954 press conference, Eisenhower explained the strategic importance of Indochina in what came to be called the "domino theory":

> You have...broader considerations that might follow what you would call the "falling domino" principle. You have a row of dominoes set up, you knock over the first one, and what will happen to the last one is the certainty that it will go over very quickly....the loss of Indochina, of Burma, of Thailand, of the Peninsula, and Indonesia following, now you begin to talk about areas that not only multiply the disadvantages that you would suffer through loss of materials, sources of materials, but now you are talking really about millions and millions and millions of people....the geographic position achieved thereby does many things. It turns the so-called island defensive chain of Japan, Formosa, of the Philippines and to the southward; it moves in to threaten Australia and New Zealand....So, the possible consequences of the loss are just incalculable to the free world. (Moss 38-39)

✦✦✦

DOCUMENT 9: The Geneva Conference

The Geneva conference was initiated by the Soviet Union and Great Britain, both of whom saw the continuation of the Indochina war as detrimental to their interests. At Geneva, the fate of Indochina was determined by the major powers rather than the inhabitants of the region. Each of the major powers had its own agenda. The Soviet Union, for example, had no geopolitical interest in Indochina. The Soviets merely wanted the war to end before they were dragged into it by their allies — the Democratic Republic of Vietnam or the People's Republic of China. With such a limited objective, their participation in the conference was minimal.

Great Britain worried that the Indochina war might spread and threaten its colonies — Malaysia and Hong Kong. It wanted to stop the spread of communism in Southeast Asia for the same reason. England began working with the United States to create an organization dedicated to stopping the spread of communism in the region. But this did not prevent the British from criticizing the United States for refusing to recognize the People's Republic of China, without whom peace in the region could not be assured. At the conference, England proposed a temporary division of Vietnam at the 17th parallel, with the Democratic Republic of Vietnam given authority over the area north of the parallel and the State of Vietnam (renamed the Republic of Vietnam in 1955) controlling the territory south of it.

France's position was greatly weakened by the fall of Dienbienphu. It nevertheless hoped to retain some political and economic influence in Indochina after the Geneva conference. The French therefore recommended that the conference limit itself to ending the military conflict and defer political/economic matters to future meetings. France resented the United States for not coming to its rescue at Dienbienphu. It was also suspicious about America's interests in Southeast Asia. France, however, saw that its interests in Indochina were tied to the United States and its willingness to lead the fight against communism in the region. At the conference, France indicated that it would support a temporary division of Vietnam along the 18th parallel, provided that a noncommunist enclave was preserved in the Red River delta near Hanoi and that the Vietnamese wishing to relocate in southern Vietnam be allowed to do so.

The United States, firmly committed to stopping the spread of international communism, believed that if any part of Indochina were placed under communist control, it would threaten to subvert all of its neighbors. It disputed the Vietminh claim that they were nationalists throwing off colonial rule. Instead, the United States saw them as pawns of communist leaders in China and the Soviet Union, whose ultimate goal was world domination. America therefore refused to recognize the People's Republic of Vietnam and maintained that the State of Vietnam was the country's legitimate government. It refused to recognize the People's Republic of China along similar lines, maintaining that the Republic of China on Taiwan was China's legitimate government. For these reasons, the United States remained somewhat aloof during the Geneva conference. It was far more concerned about establishing an international organization to defend Southeast Asia against a communist threat than to be discussing a settlement with the very people that threatened the region. At the conference, the United States called for the withdrawal of all Vietminh forces from Laos and Cambodia. It was willing to accept a temporary division of Vietnam, provided that no limits were placed on foreign assistance to defend southern Vietnam and that elections would take place no sooner than eighteen months after the division.

The People's Republic of China (PRC) was gratified to be invited to the Geneva conference despite America's refusal to recognize its legitimacy. The PRC had supported the Vietminh's struggle against the French with weapons and supplies. What the PRC desired most in 1954, however, was a respite. After its war with Japan (1937-45), its civil war (1945-49), and its intervention in the Korean War (1950-53), China needed to rebuild its social and economic institutions. It therefore tried to convince the Democratic Republic of Vietnam to accept a temporary division of Vietnam. At the conference, the PRC called for the removal of all foreign troops from northern Vietnam and accused the United States of establishing "a counterrevolutionary colonial outpost" in southern Vietnam. But for the time being, it was satisfied with having a friendly Democratic Republic of Vietnam on its southern border.

The only Indochinese delegation that played a significant role at the conference was one from the Democratic Republic of Vietnam (DRV). The PRC believed that it had earned its independence after a century of struggle. It therefore demanded that France immediately recognize the full independence and sovereignty of Vietnam, Laos, and Cambodia. The DRV insisted that all foreign troops be immediately withdrawn from these countries and that free elections be held in each of them. The DRV opposed the division of Vietnam. However, pressured by its ally, the People's Republic of China, the DRV indicated that it might accept a temporary division, provided that elections to reunify Vietnam would be held soon afterwards.

After two months of negotiations, the Geneva conference released its "Final Declarations" on July 21, 1954:

1. The Conference takes note of the Agreements ending the hostilities in Cambodia, Laos, and Viet-nam and organizing international control and supervision of the execution of the provisions of these agreements.

2. The Conference...expresses its conviction that the present Declaration...will permit Cambodia, Laos and Viet-nam henceforth to play their part, in full independence and sovereignty, in the peaceful community of nations....

4. The Conference takes note of...prohibiting the introduction into Viet-nam of foreign troops and military personnel as well as all kinds of arms and munitions. The Conference also takes note of the declarations made by the Governments of Cambodia and Laos of their resolution not to request foreign aid, whether in war materiel, in personnel or in instructors except for the purpose of the effective defense of their territory....

5. The Conference takes note...that no military base under the control of a foreign State may be established in the regrouping zones of the two parties, the latter having the obligation to see that the zones allotted to them shall not constitute part of any military alliance and shall not be utilized for the resumption of hostilities or in the service of an aggressive policy....

6. The Conference recognizes that the essential purpose of the Agreement relating to Viet-nam is to settle military questions with a view to ending hostilities and that the military demarcation line is provisional and should not in any way be interpreted as constituting a political or territorial boundary....

7. The Conference declares that...the settlement of political problems, effected on the basis of respect for principles of independence, unity and territorial integrity, shall permit the

continued

Vietnamese people to enjoy the fundamental freedoms, guaranteed by democratic institutions established as a result of free general elections by secret ballot....[G]eneral elections shall be held in July 1956, under the supervision of an international commission composed of representatives of the Member States of the International Supervisory Commission....

8. The provisions...intended to ensure the protection of individuals and of property must be most strictly applied and must, in particular, allow everyone in Viet-nam to decide freely in which zone he wishes to live.

9. The competent representative authorities of the Northern and Southern zones of Viet-nam, as well as authorities of Laos and Cambodia, must not permit any individual or collective reprisals against persons who have collaborated in any way with one of the parties during the war, or against members of such persons' families....

12. In their relations with Cambodia, Laos and Viet-nam, each member of the Geneva Conference undertakes to respect the sovereignty, the independence, the unity and the territorial integrity of the above-mentioned States, and to refrain from any interference in their internal affairs.

13. The members of the Conference agree...to ensure that the Agreements on the cessation of hostilities in Cambodia, Laos and Viet-nam are respected. (Moss 40-42)

All delegations signed the Declarations except the State of Vietnam and its new champion — the United States. The United States preferred that the French continue fighting the Vietminh with American support, even though it refused to involve its own troops in the conflict. It saw any negotiated peace that created another communist state in Asia as a defeat for the "free world." Undersecretary of State Walter B. Smith delivered America's response to the situation in Indochina on the same day the accords were delivered:

The Government of the United States being resolved to devote its efforts to the strengthening of peace in accordance with the principles and purposes of the United Nations takes note of the agreements concluded at Geneva on July 20 and 21, 1954...declares...that...it will refrain from the threat or the use of force to disturb them...and...it would view any renewal of the aggression in violation of the aforesaid agreements with grave concern and as seriously threatening international peace and security....

Concerning free elections in Viet-Nam my Government wishes to make clear its position...as follows: "In the case of nations now divided against their will, we shall continue to seek to achieve unity through free elections supervised by the United Nations to insure that they are conducted fairly."

With respect to...the State of Viet-Nam, the United States reiterates its traditional position that peoples are entitled to determine their own future and that it will not join in an arrangement which would hinder this....

We share the hope that the agreements will permit Cambodia, Laos and Viet-Nam to play their part, in full independence and sovereignty, in the peaceful community of nations, and will enable the peoples of that area to determine their own future. (Moss 42-43)

Sometime after Smith delivered this response, President Eisenhower announced that the United States was not bound to honor any part of the Geneva accords. Provisions of the Southeast Asia Treaty Organization (SEATO), created principally by the United States, also seemed to contradict the Geneva accords, particularly SEATO's protocol that extended its protection to Laos, Cambodia, and Vietnam south of the 17th parallel.

◆◆◆

DOCUMENT 10: "The Best and the Brightest"

During his 1960 presidential campaign, John F. Kennedy promised to "get America moving again." As president, he exuded youth, vitality, and confidence. Kennedy's administration reflected its leader. "It was a glittering time," journalist David Halberstam recalled, "they literally swept into office, ready, moving, generating their style, their confidence —...the word went out quickly around the Eastern seacoast, at the universities and in the political clubs, that the best men were going to Washington." Halberstam himself was caught up in the excitement:

> We seemed about to enter an Olympian age of this country, brains and intellect harnessed to great force, the better to define a common good....Day after day we read about them, each new man more brilliant than the last....There were counts kept on how many Rhodes scholars there were in the Administration.... There was a sense of involvement even for those who were not a part of the excitement. (Halberstam 50-52)

McGeorge Bundy, according to Halberstam, epitomized "the best and the brightest" men that filled Kennedy's administration. He possessed both the brilliance and the hubris of that group. Once considered for the presidency of Harvard University at age 34, Bundy became Kennedy's special assistant for national security affairs:

> He was bright and he was quick, but even this bothered people around him. They seemed to sense a lack of reflection, a lack of depth, a tendency to look at things tactically, functionally and operationally rather than intellectually; they believed Bundy thought that there was always a straight line between two points....It was the Establishment's conviction that it knew what was right and what was wrong for the country. In Bundy, this was a particularly strong strain, as if his own talent and the nation's talent were all wrapped up together, producing a curious amalgam of public interest and self-interest, his destiny and the nation's destiny....McGeorge Bundy, then, was the finest example of a special elite, a certain breed of men...linked to one another rather than to the country; in their minds they became responsible for the country but not responsive to it. (Halberstam 76)

This elitism of Kennedy's advisers concerned some veteran congressmen. When Vice President Lyndon B. Johnson expressed his excitement over meeting Kennedy's "new men" to his political mentor Sam Rayburn, he told Johnson, "Well, Lyndon, you may be right and they may be every bit as intelligent as you say, but I'd feel a whole lot better about them if just one of them had run for sheriff once." (Halberstam 53)

✦✦✦

DOCUMENT 11: The Kennedy Administration and Diem's Overthrow

In his memoir, former Defense Secretary Robert S. McNamara states, "Throughout the Kennedy years, we operated on two premises that ultimately proved contradictory. One was that the fall of South Vietnam to Communism would threaten the security of the United States and the Western world. The other was that only the South Vietnamese could defend their nation, and that America should limit its role to providing training and logistical support." (McNamara 29) The "two premises" were on a collision course in 1963, as it became clear that the South Vietnamese government could not survive without an escalation of American support. ARVN forces were being defeated in the field by NLF combatants, now supported by North Vietnamese troops. Opposition to Ngo Dinh Diem's regime was widespread, especially after Ngo Dinh Nhu's troops broke up peaceful celebrations of the Buddha's birthday and then fired on marchers protesting the crackdowns. These events embarrassed the Kennedy administration, which urged Diem to end the persecutions. Almost as a response to America's pressure, Nhu hinted that he was negotiating with Hanoi to reunite Vietnam under a neutralist government, a plan supported by French President Charles de Gaulle.

At the height of this crisis, a group of South Vietnamese generals approached CIA officers to discuss their plans to oust Diem. The generals contacted the CIA officers in order to get assurances that the United States would support their regime after a successful coup. The Kennedy administration was split on the coup. The strongest proponents of ousting Diem were Roger Hilsman, Jr., assistant secretary of state for Far Eastern affairs, Averell Harriman, under secretary of state for political affairs and Henry Cabot Lodge, Jr., America's new ambassador to South Vietnam. On August 24, 1963, Hilsman sent a cable to Lodge with the following recommendations:

> U.S. Government cannot tolerate situation in which power lies in Nhu's hands. Diem must be given chance to rid himself of Nhu and his coterie....
>
> If, in spite of all your efforts, Diem remains obdurate and refuses, then we must face the possibility that Diem himself cannot be preserved....
>
> You may also tell appropriate military commanders we will give them direct support in any interim period of breakdown central government mechanism....
>
> Concurrently with above, Ambassador and country team should urgently examine all possible alternative leadership and make detailed plans as to how we might bring about Diem's replacement if this should become necessary. (McNamara 52-53)

Harriman, according to McNamara's memoir, believed that "Diem had created a situation such that we could never achieve our objectives in Vietnam with him in control." (McNamara 64) In a September 11 cable to Washington, D.C., Lodge reported the situation in South Vietnam as "worsening rapidly" and that "the time has arrived for the U.S. to use what effective sanctions it has to bring about the fall of the existing government and the installation of another." (McNamara 65)

Those who opposed or expressed concern about the overthrow of Diem included Maxwell Taylor, chairman of the joint chiefs of staff, Secretary of Defense Robert McNamara, Secretary of State Dean Rusk, and Paul Harkins, commander of American forces in Vietnam. McNamara recalled that Hilsman's August 24 cable "shocked" Taylor: "Max knew it represented a major change in our Vietnam policy; what is more, it was totally at variance with what he believed was the proper course." (McNamara 54) McNamara agreed with Taylor. After a visit to Vietnam in late September, McNamara passed on the following observations to the president:

> The prospects that a replacement regime would be an improvement appear to be 50-50. Initially, only a strongly authoritarian regime would be able to pull the government together and maintain order....Such an authoritarian military regime...would be apt to entail a resumption of the repression at least of Diem, the corruption of the Vietnamese Establishment before Diem, and an emphasis on conventional military rather than social, economic and political considerations. (McNamara 77-78)

He therefore made the following recommendations:

> Withhold important financial support of his development programs...to impress upon Diem our disapproval of his political program....Monitor the situation closely to see what steps Diem takes to reduce repressive practices and to improve the effectiveness of the military effort....[But] we not take any initiative to encourage actively a change in government. (McNamara 78-79)

Rusk was bothered by the fact that Lodge was making strong statements against Diem without first having substantial dealings with him. He believed that Lodge was not serving as an effective conduit between Saigon and Washington, D.C. Rusk felt that this prevented Diem from comprehending the gravity of American concerns about his regime. Harkins, according to McNamara, "complained bitterly about Lodge's failure to keep him informed of coup planning, reiterated his opposition to a coup, and said he saw no alternative leader with Diem's strength of character — particularly among the generals, whom he knew well." (McNamara 82)

President Kennedy himself gave mixed messages regarding Diem's government. In an interview with CBS-TV news anchor Walter Cronkite on September 2, 1963, Kennedy stated:

> I don't think that unless a greater effort is made by the [South Vietnamese] Government to win popular support that the war can be won out there. In the final analysis, it is their war. They are the ones who have to win it or lose it....All we can do is help, and we are making it very clear, but I don't agree with those who say we should withdraw. That would be a great mistake. (McNamara 61-62)

In a September 9 interview with NBC-TV evening news anchors Chet Huntley and David Brinkley, Kennedy was asked, "have you any reason to doubt this so-called 'domino theory' that if South Vietnam falls, the rest of Southeast Asia will go behind it?" He replied, "No, I believe it.... China is so large, looms so high just beyond the frontiers, that if South Vietnam went, it would not only give them an improved geographic position for a guerrilla assault on Malaya, but would also give the impression that the wave of the future in Southeast Asia was China and the Communists." (McNamara 63-64)

After vacillating for some time, Kennedy decided that the United States "not take any initiative to encourage actively a change in government." On October 25, however, Lodge sent a cable to the White House indicating that the plans for the coup were already in their advanced stages. "Do not think," he told Kennedy's advisors, "we have the power to delay or discourage a coup." (McNamara 82) McNamara "seriously questioned whether the South Vietnamese generals would proceed with a coup if they believed the American government opposed it." Taylor agreed. He cabled Lodge: "We do not accept as a basis for U.S. policy that we have no power to delay or discourage a coup." (McNamara 82) Lodge was scheduled to leave Saigon for consultations in Washington, D.C. on November 1. The coup began before he boarded the plane. As the fighting began, Diem called Lodge:

> **Diem:** Some units have made a rebellion and I want to know, what is the attitude of the U.S.?
>
> **Lodge:** I do not feel well enough informed to be able to tell you. I have heard the shooting, but am not acquainted
>
> *continued*

> with all the facts. Also, it is 4:30 A.M. in Washington and the U.S. Government cannot possibly have a view.

Diem: But you must have some general ideas. After all, I am Chief of State. I have tried to do my duty. I want to do now what duty and good sense require. I believe in duty above all.

Lodge: You have certainly done your duty. As I told you only this morning, I admire your courage and your great contribution to your country. No one can take away from you the credit for all you have done. Now I am worried about your physical safety. I have a report that those in charge of the current activity offer you and your brother safe conduct out of the country if you resign. Had you heard this?

Diem: No. (pause) You have my phone number.

Lodge: Yes. If I can do anything for your physical safety, please call me.

Diem: I am trying to re-establish order (hangs up). (Moss 66-67)

Coup forces quickly took control of key military and communications installations in Saigon. Diem and Nhu escaped from the palace to the Chinese section of the city through an underground passage. From there, they contacted coup leaders to discuss a settlement. The troops sent to pick up the brothers shot and killed them.

America's tacit support of the coup tied it to the new regime and those that succeeded it. Looking back at Diem's overthrow, McNamara believes that the Kennedy administration "failed to confront the basic issues in Vietnam that ultimately led to his overthrow, and we continued to ignore them after his removal":

I should have forced examination, debate, and discussion on such basic questions as Could we win with Diem? If not, could he be replaced by someone with whom we could do better? If not, should we have considered working with Nhu and France for neutralization? Or, alternatively, withdrawing on the grounds that South Vietnam's political disorder made it impossible for the United States to remain there....

Dean [Rusk] — one of the most selfless, dedicated individuals ever to serve the United States — failed utterly to manage the State Department and to supervise Lodge....

And President Kennedy — whom I fault least... failed to pull together a divided U.S. government. Confronted with a choice of evils, he remained indecisive far too long. (McNamara 70)

◆◆◆

DOCUMENT 12: Gulf of Tonkin Resolution

Following alleged attacks on American destroyers by North Vietnamese torpedo boats in the Gulf of Tonkin, President Lyndon B. Johnson asked Congress to pass a resolution authorizing military action against North Vietnam. The resolution entitled "To Promote the Maintenance of International Peace and Security in Southeast Asia" (better known as the Gulf of Tonkin Resolution) was introduced in the Senate on August 5, 1964:

Whereas naval units of the Communist regime in Vietnam, in violation of the principles of the Charter of the United Nations and of international law, have deliberately and repeatedly attacked United States naval vessels lawfully present in international waters, and have thereby created serious threat to international peace; and

Whereas these attacks are part of a deliberate and systematic campaign of aggression that the Communist regime in North Vietnam has been waging against its neighbors and nations joined with them in the collective defense of the freedom; and

continued

Whereas the United States is assisting the peoples of Southeast Asia to protect their freedom and has no territorial, military or political ambitions in that area, but desires only that these peoples should be left in peace to work out their own destinies in their own way: Now, therefore, be it

Resolved by the Senate and House of Representatives of the United States of America in Congress assembled.

That the Congress approves and supports the determination of the President as Commander in Chief, to take all necessary measures to repel any armed attack against the forces of the United States and to prevent further aggression....

Sec.3. This resolution shall expire when the President shall determine that the peace and security of the area is reasonably assured by international conditions created by action of the United Nations or otherwise, except that it may be terminated earlier by concurrent resolution of the Congress. (Moss 73-74)

The resolution was shepherded through Congress by Johnson's longtime political ally J. William Fulbright. He choked off debates on the resolution and derailed attempts to amend it. A few congressmen, such as Senator Ernest Gruening and Senator Wayne Morse, expressed strong opposition to the resolution, but it passed easily — 88-2 in the Senate and 416-0 in the House:

Gruening: We now are about to authorize the President if he sees fit to move our Armed Forces...not only into South Vietnam, but also into North Vietnam, Laos, Cambodia, Thailand....That means sending our American boys into combat in a war in which we have no business, which is not our war, into which we have been misguidedly drawn, which is steadily being escalated. This resolution is a further authorization for escalation unlimited. I am opposed to sacrificing a single American boy in this venture. We have lost far too many already....

continued

> **Morse:** I believe that history will record that we have made a great mistake in subverting and circumventing the Constitution of the United States....I believe this resolution to be a historic mistake. I believe that within the next century, future generations will look with dismay and great disappointment upon a Congress which is now about to make such a historic mistake.

Historian George C. Herring called Johnson's handling of the Gulf of Tonkin incident "masterly":

> His firm but restrained response to the alleged North Vietnamese attacks won broad popular support, his rating in the Louis Harris poll skyrocketing from 42 to 72 percent overnight. He effectively neutralized [Republican presidential candidate Barry] Goldwater on Vietnam, a fact which contributed to his overwhelming electoral victory in November. Moreover, this first formal Congressional debate on Vietnam brought a near-unanimous endorsement of the President's policies and provided him an apparently solid foundation on which to construct future policy. (Herring 123)

Herring noted, however, that "the President's resounding triumph in the Tonkin Gulf affair brought with it enormous, if still unforeseen, costs." (Herring 123) Also, Senator Fulbright, who pushed the resolution through Congress, came to believe that he had been misled by Johnson on the necessity and implications of the resolution. In time, he became one of the most vocal opponents of American involvement in Vietnam on Capitol Hill.

DOCUMENT 13: Meeting to Consider the Escalation of American Involvement

Following the assassination of Ngo Dinh Diem in November 1963, a succession of generals came to power in South Vietnam, none of them with wide popular support. Seeing the weaknesses of these regimes, the National Liberation Front intensified its efforts to topple the government in the South. Soon after he became president, in November 1963, Lyndon B. Johnson was pressured to bolster the faltering South Vietnamese government and army with a major military commitment. Focusing instead on domestic programs, such as the Great Society, Johnson did not take any major action on Vietnam during the first year of his presidency. By the spring of 1965, however, Johnson's aids told him that without a significant escalation in America's military presence, the fall of South Vietnam was imminent. Johnson met with his top military and civilian advisors on July 21 and 22, 1965, to discuss the details of such an escalation. He was wary about an escalation because it might jeopardize his domestic programs. During these meetings, some of the most fundamental questions, such as the threat of a Chinese intervention and the prospect of an American victory in a protracted guerrilla war, were secretly discussed.

Secretary of Defense Robert S. McNamara began the July 21 meeting by summarizing the Pentagon's recommendation to send 200,000 troops to Vietnam by the beginning of 1966 and calling up the same number of reserves. According to their calculations, approximately 600,000 additional men would be available for duty by mid-1966.

> **George Ball** [under secretary of state]: Isn't it possible that the VC [Vietcong] will do what they did against the French — stay away from confrontation and not accommodate us?
>
> **General Earle Wheeler** [chairman of the joint chiefs of staff]: Yes, that is possible, but by constantly harassing them, they will have to fight somewhere....

continued

Ball: Mr. President, I can foresee a perilous voyage....I have...grave apprehensions that we can win under these conditions. But let me be clear. If the decision is to go ahead, I am committed.

President Lyndon Johnson: But, George, is there another course in the national interest, some course that is better than the one McNamara proposes? We know it is dangerous and perilous, but the question is, can it be avoided?...

Johnson: I can take disagreeable decisions. But I want to know can we make a case for your thoughts?

Dean Rusk [secretary of state]: What we have done since 1954 to 1961 has not been good enough. We should have probably committed ourselves heavier in 1961....

Henry Cabot Lodge, Jr. [American ambassador to South Vietnam]: There is not a tradition of a national government in Saigon. There are no roots in the country....I don't think we ought to take this government seriously. There is simply no one who can do anything. We have to do what we think we ought to do regardless of what the Saigon government does....

McNamara and Wheeler then returned to the Pentagon recommendation for more men to be sent to Vietnam. These men would give the South Vietnamese army a breathing space. No more than 100,000 would be sent at this time.

Johnson: It seems to me that you will lose a greater number of men. I don't like that.

Wheeler: Not precisely true, Mr. President. The more men we have there the greater likelihood of smaller loses.

continued

Johnson: Tell me this. What will happen if we put in 100,000 more men and then two, three years later you tell me you need 500,000 more? How would you expect me to respond to that? And what makes you think if we put in 100,000 men, Ho Chi Minh won't put in another 100,000 and match us every bit of the way?

Wheeler: (Smiling) This means greater bodies of men from North Vietnam, which will allow us to cream them.

Ball: We cannot win, Mr. President. This war will be long and protracted. The most we can hope for is a messy conclusion. There remains a great danger of intrusion by the Chinese. But the biggest problem is the problem of the long war....As casualties increase, the pressure to strike at the very jugular of North Vietnam will become very great. [If this happens, I would be] concerned about world opinion....If the war is long and protracted, as I believe it will be, then we will suffer because the world's greatest power cannot defeat guerrillas. Then there is the problem of national politics....The enemy cannot even be seen in Vietnam. He is indigenous to the country. I truly have serious doubt that an army of westerners can successfully fight Orientals in an Asian jungle....

The least harmful way to cut losses in SVN [South Vietnam] is to let the government decide it doesn't want us to stay there. Therefore, we should put such proposals to the SVN that they can't accept. Then, it would move to a neutralist position. I have no illusions that after we were asked to leave South Vietnam, that country would soon come under Hanoi control....

continued

Johnson: But George, wouldn't all these countries say that Uncle Sam was a paper tiger, wouldn't we lose credibility breaking the word of three presidents?

Ball: The worse blow would be that the mightiest power on earth is unable to defeat a handful of guerrillas.

Johnson: There are two basic troublings within me. First, that westerners can ever win a war in Asia. Second, I don't see how you can fight a war under direction of other people whose government changes every month....

Rusk: If the Communist world finds out we will not pursue our commitment to the end, I don't know where they will stay their hand. I have to say I am more optimistic than some of my colleagues. I don't believe the VC [Vietcong] have made large advances among the Vietnamese people. It is difficult to worry about massive casualties when we say we can't find the enemy. I feel strongly that one man dead is massive casualty, but in the sense that we are talking, I don't see large casualties unless the Chinese come in.

Lodge: I feel there is greater threat to start World War III if we don't go. Can't we see the similarity to our own indolence at Munich [the 1938 Munich conference where the Western Powers acquiesced to Hitler's seizure of parts of Czechoslovakia]. I simply can't be as pessimistic as Ball....We don't need to fight on roads. We have the sea. Let us visualize meeting the VC on our own terms. We don't have to spend all our time in the jungles. If we can secure our bases, the [South] Vietnamese can secure, in time a political movement....

At the July 22 meeting, Johnson reiterated his concerns about escalating America's involvement in Vietnam.

Johnson: But you don't know if 100,000 men will be enough. What makes you conclude that if you don't know where we are going — and what will happen — we shouldn't pause and find this out?

Admiral D. L. McDonald [chief of naval operations]: Sooner or later we will force them to the conference table.

Johnson: But if we put in 100,000 men won't they put in an equal number, and then where will we be?

McDonald: No, if we step up our bombing....

Johnson: Is this a chance we want to take?

McDonald: Yes sir, when I view the alternatives. Get out now or pour in more men....I think our allies will lose faith in us.

Johnson: We have few allies really helping us now....Also, why wouldn't [the North Vietnamese] call on volunteers from China and Russia?

Wheeler: ...the one thing all North Vietnamese fear is the Chinese. For them to invite Chinese volunteers is to invite China taking over North Vietnam....From a military viewpoint, we can handle, if we are determined to do so, China and North Vietnam.

McDonald: [We need to] first, supply the forces [General William] Westmoreland [who replaced General Paul Harkins as the commander of American forces in Vietnam] has asked for. Second, prepare to furnish more men, 100,000 in 1966. Third, commence building in air and naval forces, and step up air attacks on North Vietnam. Fourth, bring in needed reserves and draft calls....

continued

> **Johnson:** Doesn't it really mean that if we follow Westmoreland's requests we are in a new war? Isn't this going off the diving board?
>
> **McNamara:** If we carry forward all these recommendations, it would be a change in our policy. We have relied on the South to carry the brunt. Now we would be responsible for satisfactory military outcome.... (Williams 248-53)

◆◆◆

DOCUMENT 14: President Johnson's Dilemma

During the first two years of his presidency, Lyndon Johnson gave mixed messages on what he intended to do about Vietnam. During his presidential campaign, Johnson stated that the United States should not send troops to fight in Vietnam. On September 25, 1964, in Eufaula, Oklahoma, he said, "We don't want our American boys to do the fighting for Asian boys. We don't want to get involved in a nation with 700 million people and get tied down in a land war in Asia." On October 21, in Akron, Ohio, Johnson said, "we are not about to send American boys nine or ten thousand miles away from home to do what Asian boys ought to be doing for themselves." (Moss 77-78) Whether Johnson believed his own election campaign rhetoric or not, the realities of Vietnam were far more complex and pressing. In a 1970 interview, Johnson confided his dilemma over Vietnam to his biographer Doris Kearns, who had been a White House fellow in 1967:

> I knew from the start that I was bound to be crucified either way I moved. If I left the woman I really loved — the Great Society — in order to get involved with that bitch of a war on the other side of the world, then I would lose everything at home. All my programs. All my hopes to feed the hungry and shelter the homeless....But if I left that war and let the Communists take over South Vietnam, then I would be seen
>
> *continued*

as a coward and my nation would be seen as an appeaser and we would both find it impossible to accomplish anything for anybody anywhere on the entire globe. (Kearns 251)

Johnson ultimately decided to escalate America's involvement in Vietnam — bombing North Vietnam and sending in American combat units. Johnson explained his decision in a speech that focused on "why we are in Vietnam" at Johns Hopkins University on April 7, 1965:

Viet-Nam is far away from this quiet campus. We have no territory there, nor do we seek any. The war is dirty and difficult....

Why must we take this painful road?

Why must this Nation hazard its ease, and its interest, and its power for the sake of a people so far away?

We fight because we must fight if we are to live in a world where every country can shape its own destiny. And only in such a world will our own freedom be finally secure....

The first reality is that North Viet-Nam has attacked the independent nation of South Viet-Nam. Its object is total conquest.

Of course, some of the people of South Viet-Nam are participating in the attack on their own government. But trained men and supplies, orders and arms, flow in a constant stream from north to south.

This support is the heartbeat of the war.

And it is a war of unparalleled brutality. Simple farmers are the targets of assassination and kidnapping. Women and children are strangled in the night because their men are loyal to their government....

Over this war — and all Asia — is another reality: the deepening shadow of Communist China. The rulers in Hanoi are urged on by Peking. This is a regime which has destroyed freedom in Tibet, which has attacked India, and has been condemned by the United Nations for aggression in Korea.

continued

It is a nation which is helping the forces of violence in almost every continent. The contest in Viet-Nam is part of a wider pattern of aggressive purposes.

Why are these realities our concern? Why are we in South Viet-Nam?

We are there because we have a promise to keep. Since 1954, every American President has offered support to the people of South Viet-Nam. We have helped to build, and we have helped to defend. Thus, over many years, we have made a national pledge to help South Viet-Nam defend its independence.

And I intend to keep that promise....

We are also there to strengthen world order. Around the globe, from Berlin to Thailand, are people whose well-being rests, in part, on the

belief that they can count on us if they are attacked. To leave Viet-Nam to its fate would shake the confidence of all these people in the value of an American commitment and in the value of America's word. The result would be increased unrest and instability, and even wider war.

We are also there because there are great stakes in the balance. Let no one think for a moment that retreat from Viet-Nam would bring an end to conflict. The battle would be renewed in one country and then another. The central lesson of our time is that the appetite of aggression is never satisfied. To withdraw from one battlefield means only to prepare for the next. We must say in Southeast Asia — as we did in Europe — in the words of the Bible: "Hitherto shalt thou come, but no further...." (Williams et al., 242-43)

Interpretations of America's Involvement in the Vietnam War

by Mitch Yamasaki

Why did the United States get involved in the Vietnam War? This is a question that continues to haunt the American people, long after the last helicopter took off from the roof of the American embassy in Saigon. Leslie Gelb, a former defense department official, suggests that most nations involved in bitter wars end up examining their own traditions and values — to "see what they are made of. Are they wise and just nations? Or are they foolish and aggressive? Merciless or humane? Well led or misled?" (Gelb 14) This is certainly the case with the United States and the Vietnam War.

Interpretations of America's intervention in Vietnam are numerous and wide-ranging. "Hawks" believe, for example, that the United States had an obligation to save Vietnam from communist domination, while "doves" see the conflict as a civil war that America had no business getting involved in. Those who fought in the Vietnam War, those who lost loved ones in the war, those who directed the course of the war and those who protested against the war interpret the war differently. New evidence, the benefit of hindsight, and the simple passage of time also produce new interpretations. The following are summaries of the major interpretations of why the United States became involved in the Vietnam War.

◆◆◆

The "Official" Explanation

The "official" interpretation, or the explanation given by the administrations of Presidents Truman through Nixon, maintains that the United States was in Vietnam to stop the advance of communism. Starting with President Harry S. Truman, American leaders viewed the Soviet led "communist bloc" as a threat to the "free world." For this reason, they made the "containment" of communism a major component of their foreign policy. President Dwight D. Eisenhower believed that the fall of Indochina would lead to communist takeovers throughout Asia and the Pacific basin, a process he compared to a row of falling dominoes. John F. Kennedy affirmed his stand against international communism in his 1961 inaugural address by pledging to "pay any price, bear any burden, meet any hardship, support any friend, oppose any foe to assure the survival and the success of liberty." American policymakers also stressed the need to honor national commitments — commitments made in the effort to stop the spread of communism. When President Lyndon B. Johnson decided to escalate America's involvement in Vietnam in 1965, he reminded the American people that "we have made a national pledge to help South Viet-Nam defend its independence....To dishonor that pledge, to abandon this small and brave nation to its enemies, and to the terror that must follow, would be an unforgivable wrong."

One criticism against the official interpretation is that it unthinkingly applied lessons drawn from Europe in the 1930s to Vietnam. Historian Goran Rystad calls this the "Munich syndrome." Under the label of totalitarianism, Soviet and Chinese communism was linked to German fascism; Stalin and Mao to Hitler. This, according to Rystad, led to ideological assumptions that American policymakers consistently refused to alter: "(1) The world is bipolar, divided into the Free World and a monolithic Communist totalitarian bloc. (2) Communist regimes are inherently aggressive and Communist leaders conspire to conquer, subjugate, and dominate the Free World. (3) Local conflicts do not exist. They are testing grounds where the Communists are probing for soft spots, battles in the worldwide contention of a Cold War. (4) Appeasement and compromise are not only ineffective but disastrous and suicidal." (Kimball 58) Rystad argues that these assumptions turned anticommunism into a "religious obsession," particularly in regard to Vietnam, despite numerous indications that a unified communist bloc no longer existed in the 1960s.

The official interpretation fell out of favor after the Vietnam War. It was resurrected in the 1980s, however, by neoconservatives such as Norman Podhoretz. *In Why We Were in Vietnam* (1982), Podhoretz reiterates the position that the United States was there "because we were trying to save the Southern half of that country from the evils of Communism." To those who charge that the brutality of America's role in the Vietnam War was "worse than Communism itself," he replies that "the peoples of Indochina have, since 1975, been subjected to sufferings far worse than anything that was inflicted upon them by the United States and its allies." (197-98)

$\blacklozenge\blacklozenge\blacklozenge$

Economic Motivation

For radical historians, such as William Appleman Williams, rhetoric about saving the world from communist domination masked the real intent of American elites to capture markets and natural resources at public expense. Williams points out that the United States had been expansionist throughout its history. After conquering the western regions of the continent from the Indians and the Mexicans, Americans looked to Asia and the Pacific islands. In 1900, the United States proposed an "open door policy" towards China. The policy, according to Williams, was an attempt to gain all the advantages of economic expansion without the disadvantages of maintaining a colonial empire. Americans knew that their vast wealth and resources gave them a distinct advantage in a world open to free trade. Williams points out that the open door policy seemed outwardly docile but was actually very aggressive, using whatever means necessary to prop up or maintain governments that would do business with the United States. This accounts for America's support of ruthless dictators, such as Somosa (Nicaragua), Noriega (Panama), Marcos (Philippines), and the Shah of Iran and its often helping to put down popular uprisings against them. Noting that businessmen held key cabinet posts from the Eisenhower through the Nixon administrations, Michael Klare observes that when they could not make an "honest dollar" in their own country, American businessmen brought in the power of the federal government to secure foreign markets and raw materials at taxpayers' expense. They convinced the American people that defending their profits was in the national interest. In *At War with Asia* (1969), Noam Chomsky states that the ideology of anticommunism served as "a highly effective technique of popular mobilization in support of American policies of intervention and subversion in the post [-World War II] period":

It is an ideology adapted to an era when the civilizing mission of the white race can no longer be invoked. Thus when the United States conquered the Philippines from its own population at the turn of the century, it was stoutly bearing the White Man's Burden, whereas today in Indochina it is defending the Free World against the savage Communists.... [The goal, however, remains the same] — reduce [the economy of Asia] to part of our own economic system. (Chomsky 8-9)

◆◆◆

Arrogance of Power and Ethnocentricity

Why did American leaders ignore the ominous warnings about the dangers of America's involvement in Vietnam? Arrogance of power was Senator J. William Fulbright's answer. In a 1966 speech, Fulbright observed that "power confuses itself with virtue and tends also to take itself as omnipotence. Once imbued with the idea of a mission, a great nation easily assumes that is has the means as well as the duty to do God's work." Historian Richard Hofstadter points out that Americans, unlike Europeans, have not learned to live with even minor military setbacks, since they have only known victory. This, in Hofstadter's view, led to the "illusion of American omnipotence." "In the illusion of omnipotence, American policy-makers," according to historian Barbara Tuchman, "took it for granted that on a given aim, especially in Asia, American will could be made to prevail. This assumption came from a can-do character of a self-created nation and from the sense of competence and superpower derived from World War II." In *The March of Folly: From Troy to Vietnam* (1984), Tuchman states that this "arrogance of power" was not so much the result of "fatal hubris and over-extension" but the "failure to understand that problems and conflicts exist among other peoples that are not soluble by the application of American force and American techniques or even American goodwill." (375)

In *Backfire: A History of How American Culture Led Us into Vietnam and Made Us Fight the Way We Did* (1985), Loren Baritz notes that "America was involved in Vietnam for thirty years, but never understood the Vietnamese. We were frustrated by the incomprehensible behavior of our Vietnamese enemies and bewildered by the inexplicable behavior of our Vietnamese friends." "Our difficulties," in Baritz' view, "were not with the strangeness of the land or the inscrutability of its people....The problem was us, not them....There was something about the condition of being an American that prevented us from understanding the 'little people in the black pajamas' who beat the strongest military force in the world." At the heart of what it means to be an American is the myth of "American exceptionalism....In countless ways, Americans know in their gut — the only place myths can live — that we have been Chosen to lead the world in public morality and to instruct it in political virtue." People with customs that seem strange to Americans are seen to be in that condition "out of ignorance and poverty. They cannot help it. If they could, they would become more like us." The net result, according to Baritz, is that "we create a vision of the world made in what we think is our own image. We are proud of what we create because we are certain that our intentions are pure, our motives good, and our behavior virtuous." (6-14)

✦✦✦

Quagmire versus Stalemate Theories

Soviet Premier Nikita Khrushchev observed in 1962 that "in South Vietnam, the U.S. had stumbled into a bog. It would be mired down there for a long time." In his 1979 memoir, Henry Kissinger, who served as President Richard M. Nixon's national security director and later as his secretary of state, writes that America's "entry into the war had been the product...of a naive idealism" which was "imperceptibly gradual and progressively sobering." Historian Arthur Schlesinger, Jr. called this the "policy of one more step" which "lured the United States deeper and deeper into the morass." This analogy of stepping into a quagmire or sliding down a slippery slope was a central theme of Schlesinger's *The Bitter Heritage: Vietnam and American Democracy, 1941-1966* (1967) and was widely accepted in the 1960s and 1970s:

In retrospect, Vietnam is a triumph of the politics of inadvertence. We have achieved our present entanglement, not after due and deliberate consideration, but through a series of small decisions. It is not only idle but unfair to seek out guilty men. President Eisenhower, after rejecting American military intervention in 1954, set in motion the policy of support for Saigon which resulted, two Presidents later, in American military intervention in 1965. Each step in the deepening of the American commitment was reasonably regarded at the time as the last that would be necessary. Yet, in retrospect, each step led only to the next, until we find ourselves entrapped today in that nightmare of American strategists, a land war in Asia — a war which no President, including President Johnson, desired or intended. (31-32)

The notion that the United States inadvertently intervened in Vietnam is challenged by two former defense department analysts — Daniel Ellsberg and Leslie Gelb. Rather than stepping into a quagmire, Ellsberg and Gelb maintain that presidents knew exactly what they were getting into each time they made a decision to escalate America's involvement. They argue that the presidents did not seek victory. They merely tried to avoid defeat. Each successive administration found the political, social, and economic cost of winning the Vietnam War to be too high. Each, however, could not risk the domestic and international consequences of "losing" Vietnam to the communists. Unable either to win or lose, each administration sought a stalemate, at least until either the Vietnamese or American people grew weary of the war. Ellsberg feels that the stalemate strategy was successful until 1965 because it "cheaply" prevented a communist victory with financial assistance to the Saigon regimes and a small number of American military advisers. Gelb agrees with Ellsberg's assessment. The war-weary American people's acceptance of President Nixon's pronouncement that their nation had achieved "peace with honor" in 1973 prompted Gelb to title his book on the Vietnam War *The Irony of Vietnam: The System Worked* (1979).

Ellsberg believes that the quagmire theory has been immensely popular because "as Presidents and their partisans find comfort and political safety in the quicksand image of the *President-as-victim*, so Americans at large are reassured in sudden moments of doubt by the same image drawn large, *America-as-victim*." (Ellsberg 131) His release of secret defense department documents — the so-called Pentagon Papers — to *The New York Times* was an effort to shake the American people from what he perceived as a dangerous self-deception.

◆◆◆

Government Complicity: The Presidents and the Bureaucracy

Due to the power and autonomy given American presidents in the field of foreign policy, their attitudes and personalities played significant roles in shaping their nation's involvement in Vietnam. Some historians believe that President Harry S. Truman's ignorance in foreign affairs, deep-seated anticommunism, containment dogmatism, and crude manners brought on the Cold War. They feel that those traits also led Truman to support the French in their struggle against the Vietminh. In a meeting ten days after he became president, Truman gave Soviet Foreign Minister Vladimir Molotov a tongue-lashing. Truman later told his friend "I gave him the one-two, right to the jaw." John F. Kennedy brought a youthful spirit, charisma, and machismo to the presidency. He also brought a tendency to personalize issues, converting them into tests of will, where winning was everything. Most observers feel that Kennedy's thirst for victory and vigorous self-image was driven into him by his ambitious father — Joseph Kennedy. Some historians believe that Kennedy's brash and aggressive personality drove him to the fiasco at the Bay of Pigs, to the brink of nuclear war over missiles in Cuba, and to escalate America's involvement in Vietnam. Correspondent David Halberstam described President Lyndon B. Johnson as "the elemental man...of stunning force, drive and intelligence, and of equally stunning insecurity." Unable to emerge from the shadows of the Kennedy brothers, Johnson told his biographer Doris G. Kearns that he had "Kennedy nightmares" over the Vietnam War. In those dreams, Johnson would be tied to a cross with an angry mob approaching him. Robert Kennedy would be at the head of the mob, shouting that Johnson had betrayed his dead brother's policy on Vietnam. Halberstam feels that, in the end, machismo also played a major role in his decision to escalate

America's involvement in Vietnam. Time and again, Johnson would tell his advisers, "I am not going to be the first American president to lose a war." "So it came down to...Johnson," Halberstam writes, "reluctant, uneasy, but not a man to be backed down. Lyndon would not cut and run...no one was going to push Lyndon Johnson around." (Kimball 201)

Some historians believe that the bureaucracy was largely responsible for getting the United States involved in Vietnam. Presidents make decisions based on information and advice given to them by their national security managers. Once decisions are made, national security managers shape the manner in which they are implemented. In *Washington Plans an Aggressive War* (1971), Ralph Stavins, Richard Barnet, and Marcus Raskin assert that bureaucrats inflate and distort figures and issues in order to "induce the President to do something or to make him feel comfortable about something the bureaucracy has already done....The shrewd adviser tailors his advice to the President's prejudices as best he knows them." (Gelb 16-17) In *The Best and the Brightest* (1969), David Halberstam reveals bureaucratic duplicity in the military's assessments of the Vietnam War during the early 1960s:

> General Paul Donal Harkins [head of American military operations in Vietnam] was a man of compelling mediocrity. He had mastered one thing, which was how to play the Army game, how to get along, how not to make a superior uncomfortable....Rather than reflecting what was happening in the field, Harkins' shop reflected his Washington orders, and the facts would be fitted to Washington's hopes....There the intelligence reports were edited down by the operations people, and the Vietcong capability was always downgraded and reduced.... It was all part of the game. (227-300)

Halberstam believes that such false assessments played a significant role in the escalation of America's involvement in Vietnam.

Former state department official James C. Thomson, Jr. traces the roots of the bureaucracy's complicity back to the 1950s. Thomson recalls that his department had been "purged of its best China expertise, and of farsighted, dispassionate men, as a result of McCarthyism." Expertise and farsightedness, according to Thomson, were replaced by a need to prove one's loyalty, toughness, and machismo. Thomson remembers that "those who doubted our role in Vietnam were said to shrink from the burdens of power." Doubters and dissenters, such as Undersecretary of State George Ball, were ostracized or "domesticated." In order to avoid such a fate, many bureaucrats fell into what Thomson calls "the 'effectiveness' trap, the trap that keeps men from speaking out, as clearly or often as they might, within the government.... The inclination to remain silent or to acquiesce in the presence of the great men [the president or secretary of state] — to live to fight another day, to give on this issue so that you can be 'effective' on later issues is overwhelming." Thomson also notes that bureaucracies do not easily change their courses of action because of "human ego investment":

> Men who have participated in a decision develop a stake in that decision. As they participate in further, related decisions, their stake increases. It might have been possible to dissuade a man of strong self-confidence at an early stage of the ladder of decision; but it is infinitely harder at later stages since a change of mind there usually involves implicit or explicit repudiation of a chain of previous decisions.

In Thomson's view, it was these types of bureaucratic attitudes and behavior that largely contributed to America's involvement in Vietnam. (Kimball 217-24)

Bibliography and Suggested Further Reading

Ambrose, Stephen E., *Rise to Globalism: American Foreign Policy Since 1938*, Seventh Edition, New York: Penguin, 1993.

Baritz, Loren, *Backfire: Vietnam — the Myths that Made Us Fight, the Illusion that Helped Us Lose, the Legacy that Haunts Us Today*, New York: Ballantine Books, 1985.

Choices for the 21st Century Project, *The Limits of Power: The United States in Vietnam*, Providence: Watson Institute for International Studies, Brown University, 1994.

Chomsky, Noam, *At War with Asia*, New York: Pantheon Books, 1970.

Duiker, William, *The Rise of Nationalism in Vietnam, 1900-1941*, Ithaca: Cornell University Press, 1976.

Ellsberg, Daniel, *Papers on the War*, New York: Simon and Schuster, 1972.

Fitzgerald, Frances, *Fire in the Lake: the Vietnamese and the Americans in Vietnam*, New York: Vintage, 1989.

Gelb, Leslie H., *The Irony of Vietnam: The System Worked*, Washington, D.C.: Brookings Institute, 1979.

Halberstam, David, *The Best and the Brightest*, New York: Fawcett Crest, 1972.

Herring, George C., *America's Longest War: The United States and Vietnam, 1950-1975*, Second Edition, New York: Alfred A. Knopf, 1986.

(ed.), *The Pentagon Papers*, Abridged Edition, New York: McGraw-Hill, 1993.

Kahin, George, *Intervention*, New York: Knopf, 1986.

Kearns, Doris G., *Lyndon Johnson and the American Dream*, New York: Harper & Row, 1976.

Kimball, Jeffrey P., *To Reason Why: The Debate about the Causes of U.S. Involvement in the Vietnam War*, Philadelphia: Temple University Press, 1990.

McNamara, Robert S., *In Retrospect: The Tragedy and Lessons of Vietnam*, New York: Times Books, 1995.

Moss, George Donaldson, *A Vietnam Reader: Sources and Essays*, Englewood Cliffs: Prentice Hall, 1991.

Olson, James S. and Randy Roberts, *Where the Domino Fell: America and Vietnam, 1945-1990*, New York: St. Martin's Press, 1991.

Podhoretz, Norman, *Why We Were in Vietnam*, New York: Simon and Schuster, 1982.

Porter, Gareth (ed.), *Vietnam: The Definitive Documentation of Human Decisions*, Stanfordville: Earl Coleman Enterprises, 1979.

Starr, Jerold, ed., *The Lessons of the Vietnam War*, Pittsburgh: Center for Social Studies Education, 1991.

Schlesinger, Jr., Arthur, *The Bitter Heritage: Vietnam and American Democracy, 1941-1966*, Boston: Houghton Mifflin, 1966.

Tuchman, Barbara W., *The March of Folly: From Troy to Vietnam*, New York: Ballantine Books, 1984.

About the Editor

Mitch Yamasaki holds degrees in Asian History, European History, and a Ph.D. in American History from the University of Hawai'i, and is a Professor of History at Chaminade University of Honolulu.

He has been Chairperson of the Committee on Teaching of the Organization of American Historians; a Trustee of the National Council for History Education; a member of the National Advisory Board for the Society of History Education; and a member of the Executive Board of State Coordinators for National History Day.

When Mitch is not lecturing or writing scholarly papers, he is involved with community service projects and traveling far and wide to speak to history educators. He was honored in 1991 with the Sears, Roebuck & Co. Award for Excellence in Teaching and Campus Leadership.